Computer Networking

*The Complete Beginner's Guide to
Learning the Basics of Network
Security, Computer Architecture,
Wireless Technology and
Communications Systems (Including
Cisco, CCENT, and CCNA)*

Benjamin Walker

professional before attempting any techniques outlined in this book.

By reading this document, the reader agrees that under no circumstances is the author responsible for any losses, direct or indirect, which are incurred as a result of the use of information contained within this document, including, but not limited to, — errors, omissions, or inaccuracies.

Table of Contents

Introduction

What do you know about Computers? What do you know about Computer Networking? There are so much going on in the world. Tech is evolving every day, and the interconnections in the computer field have left us with a giant web of systems and machines interacting with one another. What makes computer technology powerful is the interconnection it fosters. Right from your phone, you can interact with your desktop computer. This connection spans in so many different ways, all at the same time. Thanks to networking, the computer has become ubiquitous. It is the very core on which our 21st-century life is premised.

The world has changed, it's either you stay on top of your game, or you end up in the dark. Staying in the loop of what is going on is the best you can do. Tech has transcended its role of revolutionizing our lives. It has become the very basis of life in the 21st century. It all started with a giant machine, numerous wires connected spanning different distances. Now, it's all a matter of bandwidth and more advanced networks.

There is so much to understand in the computer world, the widest of which is the whole Computer Network. A computer network are sets of computers which are connected for resource sharing.

This definition is as basic as it can get. However, don't be fooled; there are so many intricacies underlining this definition. Computer Networking is a whole world; it is easy to get blown away in this world. This book is culled from the immense knowledge of the author, on this subject, subjected to a grammatical breakdown which will foster an easy comprehension from you.

This text spans the whole essential elements to be understood, to the various functionalities, the wireless systems, communication, and to the more advanced concepts. In spite of the technical frameworks and structure that embellishes the Computer Networking world, this text is poised to deliver a perfect understanding of the most straightforward combination of words.

By reading this book from start to finish, your knowledge of Computer Networking is bound to attain professionalism, irrespective of its starting point. This is bound to be a long but enjoyable ride. Come along.

Hello World!

Computer Networking Defined: The Whole Concept.

What is Computer Networking?

Computer Networking is simply the formation of a computer network. A computer network can be defined as the collection of computers, printers, and other equipment that are connected (wired or wireless), with the ultimate aim of fostering communications between the devices. The process of creating this connection of devices is known as Computer Networking.

Technically, Computer Networking is referred to the process of transporting and exchanging data between points known as nodes, carried via a shared system, executed in an information system. The whole concept of Computer Networking does not consist only of the design, construction, and use of a network. It also involves the technical management, maintenance, and running of the involved infrastructure, software, and underlying policies.

In Computer Networking; systems, endpoints, and other devices can be connected, over a local area network (LAN), or a more extensive network. The larger networks, in this case, are the internet and the private Wide Area Network (WAN).

Every stakeholder (service providers, businesses, and consumers) has a role to play in ensuring that resources are effectively shared. This system of stakeholders also provides the effective use and offering of services.

Once the system involves a system responding to controls and information from a remote location, it can only be facilitated by one form of Computer Networking. Right from the making and receiving of Telephone calls, to the streaming of movies on the internet, to the internet of things. A network of Computers facilitates all.

The level of complexity of a particular network decides the skill level required to operate and maintain it. For instance, if an enterprise has numerous nodes amidst other security checks (like end-to-end encryptions), it requires an advanced level of technical administration to oversee it effectively. This is unlike the Local Area Network being utilized in a school's computer laboratory.

Components of Networking

Networking of Computers requires so many infrastructures for a seamless operation. The various types of network structures require different parts. These will be looked at extensively in the course of this book.

Physical network infrastructures are needed for a Computer Network, which includes but is not limited to; switches, routers, wireless access points, etc. There is also some underlying firmware which makes these infrastructures function correctly. Other than the physical systems, there is also the needed software deployed to monitor, manage, and secure the network.

For advanced networks, there is a need for standard protocols, which are designed to perform numerous discrete functions. These protocols are also used to communicate different data types, irrespective of the underlying hardware.

For instance, in the telephone system, a voice over IP (VoIP) can bring about the transportation of IP telephony traffic from one point to another, once these points support the protocol. This is also similar to what occurs in the browser, with the HTTP providing portals to accessing webpages. Also, over an IP based network, the IP protocols to transport data and services, since there is protocol compatibility.

Computer Networking Components Defined

As said earlier, hardware components need to be installed for the creation of a network. The fundamental elements are the Cables, Hubs, Switch, Network Interface Card (NIC), modem, and routers. In a wireless network, there is no need for cables; hence, it is eliminated.

The essential components needed for a computer network are;

- Network Interface Card (NIC)
- Hub
- Switches
- Cables and Connectors
- Router
- Modem

Computer networks range from simple to complex. However, all make use of the same essential devices and rules

- **Network Interface card (NIC)**

This is also known as the Network adapter. This is a device that enables communication between the computer and other devices involved in the network. This framework makes use of the unique hardware addresses (MAC addresses) that are encoded on the card chip. The data-link protocol then uses the MAC addresses for the discovery of other systems situated on the network, to bring about data transfer in the right direction.

The Network cards come in two types; the wired and the wireless network cards. For the wired network cards, cables and other connectors are used for the transfer of data. However, for the wireless network card, radio wave frequency technology is used. Modern laptops feature both network card types in their hardware.

- **Hub**

This is a computer networking component with the primary function of splitting network connection through to multiple computers. The hub is somewhat of a distribution center. At the request of information by a computer, from the network, the application is being transmitted to the hub through cable. When the hub receives the command, it is sent to the entire system. When this is done, each of the computers on the network is now left to decipher if the information is for them or not.

The use of a hub in the computer network used to be very vital. However, in recent times, they are getting out of use. They are now replaced by an improved communication system of devices such as the switches and routers.

- **Switch**

Switches are telecommunication devices that fall into the category of being referred to as a computer network component. Switches are basically to replace hubs, but they feature more advanced systems. Unlike the center that delivers information to every computer on a network, leaving them to figure out which owns the message. The Switch makes use of the physical device's address, which is then used to deliver the message to the right destination.

Rather than sending it out to every computer, it merely delivers straight to the destination or port. Thanks to the switch, there is a direct connection between the source and the destination. This brings about a drastic reduction in processing time. This is why in today's computer networks, we experience faster connection and processing of data.

There are some features common to both the hub and the switch. These are; Multiple RJ-45 ports, power supply, and connection lights.

- **Cables and Connectors**

Cables can transmit both media and communication. Wired networks make use of specialized cables to connect different computers on a particular network.

There are different connection types, which are;

- **Twisted pair wire:** They are classified in different categories; 1, 2, 3, 4, 5, 5E, 6 and 7. The last three types are high-speed cables that transmit data at a speed of 1gbps or more.

- **Coaxial cable:** These are more like installation cables for TVs. They are more expensive than the twisted pair wire; hence, there is the provision of faster data transmission.

- **Fiber optic cable:** These are high-speed cables that transmit data with the use of light beams through a glass bound fiber. These cables are top data transmission portals, especially when compared to the other cable types. These cables are super-fast. However, they are very costly. These cables can only be purchased and installed by the government.

- **Routers**

Routers are a common term in the computer networking ecosphere, and it is very easy to miss the clue on what it is. Many people get to use this, call the name without exactly knowing what it does and how it functions. The Router is a device used to connect a Local Area Network with the internet. The Router is the device used to share a single connection to the internet, with more than one computer in a Local Area Network.

In some cases, switches are also present in routers. Modern routers are now known to feature custom switches. Hence, when getting a router, you don't need to get a switch, especially if the LAN is only through the home or small business.

Routers come in two types; the wired and the wireless routers.

- **Modems**

Modems are devices which enables the connection of your computer to the internet over an existing telephone line. Just like the NIC, the modem is not integrated into the computer's motherboard. It is a separate device that is connected to the device once it affixed to a PCI slot on the motherboard.

A modem in its real sense does not necessarily mean a LAN. It merely connects the computer to the internet. There are several modem types. The significant difference between these modem types is the speed and transmission rate.

There are:

- Standard PC modem or dial-up modems
- Cellular modem
- Cable modem
- DSL modems

- **Gateways**

Gateways, in most cases, are misconstrued to being the same as a router. However, both entities are different. A gateway can be defined as a data communication device that fosters the provision of a remote network with connectivity to a host network.

Gateways are designed to provide communication to remote networks or autonomous systems that are out of bounds for the host network nodes. In simple terms, the gateway can be defined as the entry and exit point of a particular network. Every data that is going in and out of a specific network of computers first interacts with the gateway. This is so that they can be allowed to use to routing path.

Routers are being categorized as gateway devices because they are designed to perform this function to computer networks.

Computer networks (LAN or WAN) are always limited in their reach. They basically can easily interact with the other computers in the system. Whenever there is a need to interact with another computer or a node on another system, then a gateway is needed. Routers are specific, in that they are portals with which a computer network communicates with the internet. Gateways might be portals to another Local Area Network.

Other than the routing of data packets, gateways are also designed to possess information about the host network's internal paths and the learning paths of other networks. When there is a need for the network node to communicate with another external network, the packet of data has to pass through the gateway. The gateway then routes the data to the right destination.

Network bridges

Network bridges are computer networking devices that are designed to create the aggregation of the network from different communication networks. This is a process known as network bridging. This might be confused with routing; however, there are fundamental differences.

Routing as a process involves the communication of different networks, while they remain distinct. However, bridging consists of the communication of separate networks, carried in a manner that depicts singularity.

The term wireless bridging is culled in the case where one or more of the connected networks are wireless.

Network bridging is of three types. These are the simple bridging, multiport bridging, and learning bridging.

• Learning or transparent bridging

In the transparent or learning bridging, a table called the forwarding information base is used in the control of frames between network segments. At the start of a network, the tables are empty but are subsequently filled as there is the reception of frames.

Whenever the destination address is not found on a table, the frame is transferred to the other ports of the bridge. They are flooded to the other ports, other than the port from which it emanated. During this flooding process, a host is created on the destination network, with the subsequent creation of a forwarding database entry.

For this process to be completed, both the source and destination address needs to be known. The source address is recorded in the table, while the destination addresses are searched for in the table, which is then matched to the proper segment to which the frame is sent.

This system is designed to be somewhat of a filter. If the frame's destination is read, the bridge then decides if the next action is to forward it, or to filter it. The bridge will only transmit the data if the destination is on another segment of the network. However, in the case where the destination is in the same section as its source, it is being filtered. This filtration process prevents the date from entering into another segment; it will be irrelevant.

This technology was developed as far back as 1980, by the Digital Equipment Corporation. This type of bridging can be operated on devices with more than two ports.

- **Simple bridging**

In the case of simple bridging, two networks are connected. This connection is made by a transparent operation, in which the bridge decides on a frame-to-frame basis, which information to forward from one system to another. The simple bridging process is as simple as it can get, making use of a store and forward model.

In the course of the transfer, there is the verification of the source network, and there is the advent of CSMA/CD delays on the destination network. Another effect of this bridge is that it creates a collision domain on either side of the bridge. This facilitates a drastic reduction in a collision.

- **Multiport bridging**

This type of bridging connect several networks, and they also operate transparently. This is to decide a frame-to-frame basis with which traffic is being forwarded. This system is also needed to determine the destination to forward traffic. Just like the simple bridging, the multiport system also makes use of the store and forward operation. The multiport bridge function is performing the role of network switching.

Methods of Forwarding

Forwarding is the process with which the bridge passes a data link next frame from the source to its destination. Four forwarding methods can be used by a bridge, which are;

- **Store and forward:** In this method, the frames are buffered and verified before they are being forwarded. In this case, however, the entire structure is first received before it is passed to its destination.
- **Cut through:** For the cut through, the switch begins forwarding the frames, immediately it receives information on the destination. This method is fast but is devoid of error checking. However, when there is too much traffic on the outgoing port, then it falls back to the store and forward method. Another case where the bridge reverts to the store and forward method is when there is a higher speed of processing at the egress port than the ingress port.
- **Fragment free:** This method is crafted to maximize the advantage of both of the initially stated methods. This bridge checks for the first 64 bytes of the

frame. It is in this first 64 byte that the address information is stored. According to specifications by Ethernet, collisions should also be detected in this span. Hence, whenever there is a collision in the first 64 frames, the frame will not be forwarded. Error checking is however left for the end device.

- **Adaptive switching:** This is a more advanced method in which the bridge automatically chooses between any of the methods above.

Networking Topologies

You might wonder what network topologies are. It is merely a term used in the description of the schematic depiction of the arrangement of a network. It is used to describe the various ways in which nodes are connected.

Here is a rundown on the different ways in which computers are connected to a network.

Bus Topology

In the bus topology, all the computers on the network are connected to a single cable. When this connection is made such that there are only two endpoints, then it is referred to as the Linear Bus Topology.

Features of Bus Topology

- The bus topology ensures the transmission of data in only one direction

- In this connection, all computers are connected to a single cable.

Advantages of the Bus Topology

- The bus topology as we know it is very cost-effective
- This topology system makes use of the least amount of cable, unlike the others
- This is sufficient for small networks
- A layperson can easily understand this system
- You can also quickly expand on this network.

Disadvantages

- Once there is a problem in one part of the cable, the whole network is down
- At the advent of traffic on the network, the entire network will have a slowed-down performance
- There is a limit to the strength of the cable
- This topology is not as speed effective as the ring topology.

Ring Topology

Just as the name implies, the connection between the computers causes them to end up forming a ring. The very last of the computer in this ring is then connected to the first. In this connection, each computer gets to have two neighbors.

Features of the Ring topology

-    In the ring topology several nodes, repeaters are used.

-    The transmission, in this case, is unidirectional. There are some cases it can also be bidirectional, with the presence of 2 connections between each network node. This is called the Dual ring topology.

-    For the dual ring topology, there is the formation of two ring networks. Here, data flows in the opposite direction. When there is the failure of one ring, the second ring gets to act as the backup. This way, the network doesn't crash, which is unlike the bus topology.

-    There is the transfer of data in sequence. The data transmitted in this network passes through each node of the network until it gets to the destination.

Advantages of ring topology

-    High traffic, in this case, does not affect the transfer of data. This is because transmission of data is only possible at nodes with tokens

-    This system of computers is very cheap to install

Disadvantages of Ring Topology

-    It is not easy to troubleshoot this network of computers

-    When there is the addition or removal of computers, network activity is always disturbed

-    When one computer fails, it disrupts the whole network

Star Topology

In the star topology, computers are connected to the cable through a single hub. The hub, in this case, acts as the central node, as the other nodes are connected to it.

Features of the star topology

- There is the presence of a dedicated connection to the hub for every node
- The hub is also the repeater that allows for data flow
- The star topology can be used with twisted pair, Optical fiber or coaxial cable.

dvantages of Star Topology

- You can be sure of fast performance on this connection, as there are few nodes and a reduced traffic
- You can easily upgrade the hub
- It is not difficult to troubleshoot
- You can easily set this system up, or modify it
- When one node fails, it does not affect the other nodes.

Disadvantages of Star Topology

- Installing this system is not cost-effective
- Usage is also expensive
- Since there is a dependence on the hub, once the hub fails, the network stops

\- Performance of the system is based on the hub, which in turn is dependent on its capacity.

Mesh Topology

This is a point connection to nodes or devices. Every node is connected to the other. The Mesh technology has two main techniques, which are; Routing and Flooding.

\- Mesh Topology: **Routing**

In the system of routing, there is a custom logical system used, which is based on the requirements of the network. One way is to ensure that data reaches its destination through the shortest possible channel. There is also how the routing logic is aware of any broken link in the network and makes sure to steer clear of such breaks. It is also possible to create a logic routing that can repair the broken nodes.

\- Mesh Topology: **Flooding**

In this case, the same information is transmitted to all the nodes on the network. This cuts the rope on the need for a routing logic. This network is somewhat robust, and data security is more ensured. However, loads pile on this network.

There are two main types of Mesh Topology, these are;

1. **Partial Mesh Topology:** The connection in this mesh system is similar to the conventional style; however, some devices only get connected to two or three other devices

2. **Full Mesh Topology:** This is a connection in which each device is connected to every other device in the network.

Features of the Mesh Topology

- There is a full connection between every device
- It is a very robust networking system
- It is not flexible

Advantages of Mesh Topology

- Each connection is designed to be the Carrier of its load of data
- It is robust
- You can easily identify faults
- There is the provision of security and privacy

Disadvantages of Mesh Topology

- Installation and Configuration is complicated
- The cost of cable acquisition is much
- You will need bulk wiring

Tree Topology

In this system of computer networking, there is a root node to which all other devices are connected to.

This brings about hierarchy. Another name for this system is "hierarchical topology." For a connection to be categorized like this, there must be the presence of at least three hierarchy.

Features of the tree topology

- This is the best system of connection in workstation
- This is preferably used in a Wide Area Network

Advantages of Tree Topology

- This is an extension of the bus and star topologies
- Whenever you want it, you can expand on the nodes
- This network system can be easily managed and maintained
- You can quickly carry out error detection

Disadvantages of Tree Topology

- There is a massive volume of cable needed
- It is a costly network to set up
- Whenever you add more nodes, the cost of maintenance is upped
- When the central hub fails, the whole network is gone

Hybrid Topology

The Hybrid Topology can be somewhat tricky, as it is slightly a system of two topologies that each emanate from two or more topologies.

Features of hybrid topology

- There is a combination of two or more topologies
- It always inherits the upside and downside of the topologies involved

Advantages of hybrid topologies

- This is a reliable format as you can easily detect errors
- It is very effective
- The size is scalable
- The design is very flexible

Disadvantages of hybrid topologies.

- The design is flexible but very complex
- There is a significant burden on the cost

Computer Networking is a whole world on its own. The profound effect it has had on the way we communicate amidst ourselves. It all started with systems that were created to allow for government researchers and military leaders to function more effectively. However, advancement has created a world web of devices, becoming the very basis of life.

Chapter 1: Types of Computer Networking

The introductory part of this book has seen us adequately describe what we mean by Computer Networking. We also took an in-depth dive into the various components that are essential to the computer network. We took a look at bridges and topologies, all of which are vital to Computer Networking. It is a giant network of devices, which fosters communication.

These connections are also categorized, and these classes are culled based on size, distance, and structure. We would take these different network types in sequence, reaching deep into what each entails. Sit back, have a cup of coffee close to you, enjoy.

Local Area Network (LAN)

You must have heard of this somewhere, and if you haven't, you have been informed. Local Area Networks are simply a connection of computer systems and devices, spanning a small area. More often than not, you will see a LAN connected just across a room, building or group of buildings,

Beyond the small area of connection, one LAN can be connected to another through telephone lines and radio waves. When this connection is however made, it takes away the moniker "Local Area Network," taking up "Wide Area Network." This is the fundamental difference between a LAN and the WAN. WAN extends over a more extensive distance, and it comprises of more than one Local Area Network.

Nodes of a LAN

Don't be mistaken between a LAN and the WAN. LAN is merely a connection between workstations and personal computers. In the Local Area Network, each node (which is the computer) has a CPU. This CPU is then used to execute programs, and it also has an extended function of accessing data and devices on other parts of the network. With the Local Area Network, tools and data can be shared seamlessly. Imagine a scenario in which you have more than one computer in your business space, but as a startup, you cannot afford to buy more than one colored printer. Thanks to LAN, you can share the colored printer across all the computers.

Via the LAN, users can also communicate with themselves. The LAN permits users to engage in chat sessions or send emails. You must have seen this in high school movies where the guy messages the girl via the school's computers, during a practical computer session. That is the Local Area Network at work.

On the LAN, data can be transmitted at lightning speed, way faster than data can be sent on telephone lines. LAN is fast, there is no doubt about that, but you should know this is dependent on the distance we are talking about. Another factor that can affect this speed is the number of the computer on the LAN.

Types of a Local Area Network

Local Area Networks are of frequent use, but the Ethernet is the most popular one. The Macintosh Computers by Apple have an AppleTalk Network System built into them. This creates the Apple Macintosh Networks.

As a statement of fact, LAN differs, and this difference is based on these characteristics.

- **Topology:** This has been described earlier as the way devices on a network are arranged. The various systems are explicitly defined in the introductory part of this book.

- **Protocols:** We would get more in-depth about protocols in the latter part of this book. They are the set of rules and encoding specifications that are followed for the transfer of data. These protocols are designed to determine whether a network makes use of the peer-to-peer or client/server architecture. The peer-to-peer and client/server architectures are also further explained in this text.

- **Media:** This refers to the medium in which the devices are being connected. Twisted-pair wires, coaxial cables, or fiber optic cables can be used. However, you should note that some Local Area Network no longer makes use of the cables, but make use of radio waves.

Deploying a Wireless LAN

Implementing Wireless networks nowadays is as easy as cheese. It completely topples the need to use wires across distances. In deploying wireless technology, the very first thing you need to do is to confirm that the standard of wireless networking you want. You don't want to choose any standard, as this it must be able to support your network access points, routers and the wireless network interface cards to be used for your computers and network resources.

Wide Area Network (WAN)

This is a geographically distributed private network telecommunication network that fosters a connection between two or more Local Area Networks (LAN). Remember that LAN is simply a connection of computers across a relatively small distance. However, the WAN is a more extensive network. One excellent example is the consideration of an enterprise with a headquarters and other branches, as well as some other linked facilities. The WAN is going to be a connection between the various LAN established in each of these locations.

The connection between different LANs is fostered by the use of a router or a gateway device. WAN is mostly used across enterprises, and it allows for applications, services, and other centrally located resources. Thanks to the WAN framework, the need for installation of the same application server across different locations of an enterprise, is eliminated.

Unlike LAN, WAN is not limited to a particular location. This is because the WAN is premised on a LAN, which can be individually located in different places, irrespective of the distance.

A Virtual Private Network ensures connection and security on the WAN. There are different types of VPNs, and they are all used in different situations. The IPsec VPN is most commonly used for site-to-site connections. Such as the one established between the branch office and the headquarters.

The SSL VPNs is more commonly used, as it allows for remote access for individual access. This is possible, having ensured that data from an individual over the network is encrypted.

Other than these VPNs, the linear fiber optic can also be used. This, unlike the others, offers better performance, reliability, and security. More often than not, enterprises are not able to afford this type of connection.

Types of WAN connections – and how they work.

The wan connection can either be wired or wireless. On the wired WAN service, you can find the multiprotocol label switching, T 1s, Carrier Ethernet, and commercial broadband internet links. On the other hand, the wireless WAN can feature the 4G LTE, the 5G, public Wi-Fi, and the satellite networks.

For most enterprises out there, the wired network connection is still the most preferred. However, thanks to the 4G and the 5G, the wireless connection is gaining traction, and it is only a matter of time before the wired connections are out of date.

The infrastructure needed to run the WAN framework can be privately owned, and a third party can provide the service. Third parties like telecommunication carrier, internet service provider, private IP network operator, and cable provision companies. Either a complete owner or shared ownership is possible to operate the Wide Area Network. For the hybrid WAN frameworks, there is a combination of both private and public network services.

For ease of use and deployment on the part of the enterprises, the Software-defined WAN (SD-WAN) are being designed. With this framework on the ground, enterprises can quickly deploy, operate, and manage their systems.

Two primary functions can be performed by the software platforms or customer premises equipment (CPE). These functions are thanks to the combination of virtualization, on-site SD-WAN devices, network overlays, and application-level policies. These functions are;

- The aggregation of multiple private and public WAN links
- The automatic selection of the most optimal route for traffic, which is based on prevalent conditions.

For the second function to be achieved, network managers have been required to manually reconfigure their networks, when they wish to reroute the traffic to multiple routes.

WAN Optimization

Performance in a Wide Area Network can receive a big blow, mainly caused by latency and bandwidth constraint. To combat this, there are WAN optimization devices created. These devices have several techniques with which they work. These techniques are; deduplication, compression, protocol optimization, local caching, and traffic shaping.

Also, with the SD-WAN or CPE platforms, you get a higher level of performance control. These work by providing lower-cost bandwidth connections. This is achieved in the form of the commercial mode of connection to the internet. Reliability is also ensured thanks to traffic shaping and tools designed to maintain quality of service.

WAN Security

Security in the WAN framework needs to be localized. It should be expanded to where the end-users are located. Even if they make use of the network from their home. If you are going to make use of the WAN network, you need to make use of firewall and antivirus software. With these, you can prevent unauthorized access or hacks by other persons or devices.

VPN is a system that allows for connection to a WAN, but it also provides an added layer of encryption, which can lead to anonymity. It is best to connect to a WAN with the use of a VPN. Irrespective of where the connection is being made, the use of CPN is essential. Security needs to be beefed in enterprises, especially if you are involved in one. Remember that sometimes ago, a hacker got into Microsoft systems by gaining access to an employee's home computer. This way, he was able to follow the VPN back to the Microsoft HQ.

Advantages and Disadvantages of the Wide Area Network

WAN is the best way to go for large enterprises and systems. There are several benefits to this network of devices, which include;

-   The WAN can reach an extensive geographical location
-   It is a centralized infrastructure
-   The security detail is more than the local area network
-   There is an increased span in bandwidth

The downsides include;

-   It is costly to set up this network
-   The system is very prone to breach and hacks
-   To maintain security on this network, there is the need to spend more on antivirus software and firewalls.

Metropolitan Area Network (MAN)

The Metropolitan area network is a somewhat more extensive network than the Local Area Network. This network is more significant than the LAN, but it is not as comprehensive and broad as the LAN. In most cases, this involves the interconnection of networks within a city, which also provides an internet connection.

Factors that distinguish the Metropolitan Area Network

Several factors set the MAN apart from the other networks.

-   The size of the network ranges from 5 to 50 km. This network represents an area as wide as it is on campus, and it could go as wide as a whole city – take New York, for example.

- The rate of data transmission is somewhat fast.

- In most cases, a user can own a MAN, and a network provider can also hold it. The network provider, in turn, sells services to users. This is unlike the practice in LAN, where the service is to one organization

- With the MAN< sharing regional resources is also possible.

Efficiency and speed are the main features of the Metropolitan Area Networks. They make use of the fiber optic cables. This network system is ideal for many users, as it is a medium-sized network. When speed is prioritized in the connection to be built, this is the ideal network to be adapted for use.

Chapter 2: Wired Network Technology

In recent times, wireless technologies have taken over the mainstream of how we connect, and how we connect computers. However, there is still wired technology in adoption. If not anything, think of the use of the HDMI cord in connecting projectors to the screen. Think of the use of the USB cord to connect your phone to your computer. These are just a few examples of the various ways in which wired technology is still being used.

It is possible to wonder why this technology is still in use, why can't we switch to wireless connections across all devices. Well, with the advent of 5G, more devices will switch to the wireless connection, but the chances of that eradicating wireless connection may somewhat be impossible. The chances of wired technologies persisting longer remain.

The use of wired technology comes with its advantages and disadvantages, which will be looked at in this chapter. However, what is the wired network technology all about?

Wired Network technology

Connections between devices that are other than wireless are all wired. These connections are designed to involve the use of cables, while wireless connections are carried via radio waves and frequencies. With a physical cable, data is being transferred between different devices and computer systems.

Wired networks are the common type of wired configurations out there. The vast majority of the wired cables out there make use of the Ethernet cable to foster the transfer of data between points. An example of a simple wired connection is when a router is connected across computers. On a more extensive network, several routers and switches are involved, to foster the overall connection of all devices on the network.

With the use of cable on a wired network for the internet, a computer is connected to a cable modem, a T1 line or other types of internet connection. This then provides the internet data to all the other devices connected across the network.

Wired network technology also involved some peripheral connections, of which the connection of keyboards and mice with USB fall under. Though some of these connections are wireless already, there are still wired connections.

On the flip side, the connection between monitors and external drives is not categorized as wired networks. This is because there are no alternative wireless connections. You can only have wired connections for these, for now. It's simple; a connection is only categorized as a wired network if there are wireless alternatives.

Other peripheral wired, as said earlier, are now wireless. However, some users prefer the use of the wired ones, which is due to some perceived advantages over the wired ones. One such advantage is seen in the Ethernet connections. When you are using the internet over an Ethernet connection, it is not prone to signal interference. However, with the Wi-Fi, this is possible and happens a lot.

It might seem hard to believe, but wired connections are always faster than the wireless counterparts. This is because there is a faster transfer of data through the mechanical medium than there is with the electromagnetic mediums. So, if you are browsing, it is faster with the Ethernet cable than with Wi-Fi.

Also, with wired peripheral devices, you need not replace components or the device as a whole, frequently. On the wireless mouse, you are always required to replace the batteries. This doesn't happen with the traditional wired mouse.

Another advantage is in the case of heavy-duty activities like gaming. Gamers prefer to use wired mouse and keyboards than the wireless one, all in a bid to reduce latency to zero. Wireless gears are prone to latency, which is not possible with the wired gears.

Types of Wired Network Media

Wired connection is always done with the use of a media, and there are three common types of these.

- Twisted-pair cable
- Coaxial cable
- Fiber-optic cable.

There are slight differences in how these wired medium function and they are all adapted to different functions. For the twisted-pair media, they accept signals and data in the form of electric current, while the optic-fiber cables receive theirs in the form of light.

- **Twisted pair cable**

This media is composed of two conductors, and each of these conductors is coated with insulators, while twisted together. These wires function differently, as one is used for the conduction of signals to the receiver, while the other is used for ground reference.

One downside to the use of this cable type is that it is prone to interference and cross-talks that can bring about unwanted signals in the transmission. There are two main types of the twisted pair cable, which are;

- **Unshielded twisted pair cable:** These are known to consist of two insulating copper wires. The copper wires in this cable pair are coiled around one another in a helical form. This causes a reduction in the electrical interference from a similar pair. These wires are always colored to aid the identification of the various wires. These wires are known to be of a high-speed capacity, and the high-grade models are used extensively in Ethernet technologies.

However, these wires are unfortunately of a lower bandwidth, especially when compared to the Coaxial cables. And it is very prone to interference.

-   **Shielded Twisted Pair Cable:** These cable types are made of metallic foil or braided meshes. The metal casing around the wires helps it reduce electromagnetic noise. This also prevents cross-talk, offers more speed the unshielded and coaxial cables. Either it is analog transmission or digital transmission, these wires can be effectively used. The downside is that manufacturing is not easy.

• **Coaxial Cable**

This cable goes by this name due to the presence of two conductors arranged such that they are parallel to one another. In this cable, copper is used as the central conductor, while a layer of PVC surrounds it. The use of metallic as the outer wrap is to prevent noise and keep off other conductors. The outer conductor, in this case, is wrapped in an insulating sheath.

The use of coaxial cable comes with its benefits. If you are looking for the best cable for telephone lines, this is the best. These cables can transmit digital signals at a very high speed of 10Mbps. Another high point to the use of this cable is that there is an improved level of noise immunity, as compared to other cables. Thanks to the improved shielding of the cable, it can travel long distances at a very high speed.

There is, however, some downside to these cables. The whole network is prone to failure at the failure of a single cable. Also, you can experience the ground loop, especially if the shielding is not perfect.

- **Fiber optic cable**

This cable type is made of plastic or glass, and it is designed to transmit signals in the form of light. In this cable, there is the movement of light only in one direction. In the case where two-way communication is needed, there needs to be a second communication enacted between the two devices. Basically, the optical fibers are mainly for the guidance of light through a channel.

In the optic fiber cables, there is something called the fiber-optic cable connector. There are three types of this connector, which are;

- Subscriber channel connector – used for cable TV. This uses a push/pull system of the lock.
- Straight tip connector – used for connection to networking devices
- The MT-RJ connector which makes use of two fibers and integrates them in just one design

The advantages of using the optic fiber connector are; its resistance to corrosion and the level of immunity to tapping. The downside, however, is that there is the presence of unidirectional propagation of light.

Advantages of using a wired network

So much has been said about the wired network, and how it works. However, if you are one that is all caught in the frenzy of having a connection between devices as wireless, it might be hard to see the essence of having a wired connection. I'm sure you are hoping that monitor connected to the CPU ends up becoming wireless, entirely.

What you should know is that wired connections have some advantages over the wireless counterparts. These edge has not been attained by the wireless connections, which has ensured the persistence of the wired devices. Here are some advantages you should take note of;

- **It is very reliable and stable**

If your wired network has been set up by a professional, you can be sure of stability and reliability. Every wired connection has intrinsic components that need to be correctly connected to ensure proper functionality. Components like the hubs, switches, and Ethernet cables. Once these components are perfectly in sync, you can be sure of a network system that works like a horse. With the advent of the 5G and subsequent developments that will follow (as seen in the case of the Wi-Fi 6), wireless network will get better. But, as it stands and with improvement on hardware, wired connections are more stable.

Another factor that aids the reliability and stability of the wired network is that it is devoid of any interference from other connections. For instance, in the case of wired connections that are situated close to one another, you cannot experience any interference. However, such proximity will most likely cause interference in wireless systems.

Also, the presence of obstacles like walls and other objects causes a waning of the wireless network connection. In the case of the wired network, irrespective of the distance or obstacles, speed, and the optimal connection is maintained.

- **Visibility**

In a wired connection, you can be sure of the network's privacy, such that a particular network is not visible to another network, except they are connected. When the nodes are connected, there is the facilitation of an effective data transfer. All that is needed for different networks to communicate are the nodes. Once the nodes are connected, they can recognize other nodes in the system and ensure that the right data is delivered to the correct node.

- **Speed**

Speed is another advantage of the wired network. As of now, wireless networks cannot be compared to the wired networks in terms of speed. In the wireless connection, there is the probability of the presence of dead spots. These are not present with wired connections. Wired connections are devoid of dead spots because different cables are used to have devices connected to the network. This arrangement brings about the transfer of data to individual devices on the network.

Another factor that contributes to the speed of the wired network is that there is no unnecessary traffic that can weigh on the network. With the use of a cable, an unauthorized user cannot connect to the network.

- **Security**

Security comes easier on the wired network than it does on the wireless network. Once you ensure that the firewall is secure, coupled with other security applications, you can be assured of security. Once you ensure the proper connection of the ports and the network is continuously monitored, there is a drastic reduction in security breaches and harms. This advantage is needed in institutions with numerous and sensitive transactions going on daily.

- **Cost**

This is another area the wired connections beat the wireless networks. The cost incurred in the development of a wired network for your institution is all dependent on the specific framework you are installing. Irrespective of the type of framework you are up for, the cost is always going to be lesser than that needed for the wireless network.

The various components to be used on the wired network, such as; Ethernet cables, switches, routers, etc. all come at a meager price. Also, unlike the wireless network, there is a reduction in the need for incessant upgrades. The hardware used in building this wired framework always stands the test of time.

Disadvantages of the wired network

The advantages of the wired network are numerous and make it worth considering. But does that make it the perfect networking system? If it has been, there will most likely not be the development of the wireless systems. There are several downsides to the wired network, which are;

- **It is not mobile**

You can't carry your wired routers around just as you can take your mobile Wi-Fi around. Wired networks are, unfortunately, inflexible in the aspect of mobility. Whatever location you are going to use your network, there has to be a cable connected to that point. Think of it as something like this, once your wired connection has an outlet in your living room, the only way to access that network is while in your living room and not in the bedroom.

In many cases, this might not be a big deal, especially in an office setting where there are no constant shifts in positions of devices.

- **Installation**

The installation is cheaper, that's a given, but it takes too much time to get it done. This is because more components are needed, and getting them in sync can be an enormous task. Other than the number of components that need to be connected, another factor that influences the duration of installation is the size. The bigger the network infrastructure you want to install, the longer it takes.

- **Maintenance**

If your network is small, you might not need a server. However, on the expansion of the network, there is a need for a server. The server is designed to handle connectivity, capacity, storage, and workload. Once this need arises, the cost of maintenance is sure to skyrocket. Beyond paying for the server and the cost to have it always running, you will need and hire and pay professionals to oversee it daily.

- **Wires**

When the number of cables required to foster a connection becomes so much, it may be tough to control, and it can be annoying. Imagine having wires litter the ground and walls. Managing the clumsiness and bulkiness that comes with a wired connection may be hard, and it is better to stay off it.

The wired technology has been in existence for quite some time, and truth be told, it has served well. The advantages of using the wired network are so concrete that the inconvenience it comes with may be overlooked.

Chapter 3: Functionality of Wireless Network

How soon do you think it will take before all our device connections all turn wireless? Slowly but steadily, technological innovations are doing away with the need for wires to connect two devices. Out of the context of networking (but surely with the use of wire), let's take a close look at smartphones that now have wireless charging. It had always seemed to be impossible, but now it is. Your phone needs to be on a device, and energy is being transmitted. That's just surreal, but it's technology at work.

Wireless technology started being a thing since the early '90s, and over the century, it has gotten better, faster, and more reliable. As discussed earlier, the wired network still has some advantages over the wireless network. But, these edges can be ignored (especially if you can get things done relatively fast with the wireless technology).

We have defined the wired technology, and it has been established that the other form of connection other than the wired systems, is the wireless system. They are not mutually exclusive to one another.

What is the wireless network? The name has some hint, but is that all there is to it? – A system of connection without the use of wires.

What exactly is the wireless system?

Technically, a wireless system can be defined as one that makes use of radio waves in the transmission of signals and data, as opposed to the use of wires and cables. The wireless networks have undergone so much innovation and development to function just like a phone. To use your phone, you don't need to connect to a phone line; this is precisely the same with the wireless network.

You don't need to mechanically connect with a wireless computer network before you can use the network.

Setting up a wireless network is simple, but there are some fundamentals you need to understand.

• The very common name for the wireless network is the WLAN – Wireless Local Area Network. In some cases, people prefer the use of LAWN – Local Area Wireless Network. The wireless networks are sometimes wrongly referred to as Wi-Fi. In actuality, the Wi-Fi is just one form of the wireless network. The Wi-Fi is the 802.11b standard.

• The name of the wireless computer network is the SSID. The SSID is the acronym for Service Set Identifier. Hence, for a computer to have access to a particular network, it must have the SSID as the other computers in the network. This SSID is always unique to particular computer networks.

• It is possible for there to be transmission by a particular network, across different channels. To ensure the seamless communication between several computers on a specific network, they must be configured to transmit data via the same channel.

• A wireless computer network can have as low as two computers connected by wireless network adapters. This network type is referred to as the ad-hoc made network.

• There is also a more sophisticated form of network referred to as the infrastructure mode network. There is no big deal to the network actually. It merely refers to a situation in which a group of wireless computers is connected, and also be connected to an already existing cabled network. The connection to the cabled network is enabled by the use of a wireless access point (WAP).

With the use of the wireless network, enterprises can cut down on cost of trying to introduce cables into buildings and across distances. The very basis of the wireless connections are radio waves, which is an implementation that is carried out at the physical level of the network's framework.

There are four main types of the wireless network (which we will take an in-depth look into, during this book);

• **LAN:** The wireless local area network; which connects several devices across a given location, but without the use of cable. The connection can also be made to the internet

- **MAN:** The wireless Metropolitan area network; which is the connection of several LANs
- **WAN**: The wireless Wide area network; which is the connection of large areas such as cities and towns
- **PAN:** The wireless personal area network; which is an interconnection of devices over a short span, just for a personal user.

Note this; every connection done without the need for cables (but that has the cabled alternatives) are referred to as the wireless networks.

Wireless Technology Standards

Wireless technology is just as it sounds. Remember that I said wireless networks are always wrongly referred to as Wi-Fi and that Wi-Fi is only one of the different forms of wireless networks. It is just one of the ways with which a computer can connect to the internet. For the sake of this book and so you don't get confused, we will use both terms (Wi-Fi and wireless networks) interchangeably.

Before we continue, know this, Wi-Fi is simply an acronym for wireless fidelity

There are different Wireless Networks (or Wi-Fi) standards out there. The various devices you own, such as the router, tablet, smartphone, and smart home devices all have a means with which they connect to the internet. The Wireless network standards are continually changing, within the space of a few years. There are always updates, and these updates are what bring about faster internet, improved connectivity, and seamless handling of simultaneous connections.

What are wireless network standards? You will ask. These are just a set of services and protocols that define the functionality of your Wi-Fi network and other data transmission networks.

There are different types of wireless network standards, and as said, new versions are released from time to time. You can see these versions as updates. The most common types nowadays are the IEEE 802.11 wireless LAN & Mesh.

This particular Wi-Fi standard is always updated every few years. The most current update is the 802.11ac, while the 802.11ax is just jumping into the mainstream of wireless connection in the world.

The various forms of the Wireless standards

IEEE 802.11: This was originally created in 1997. It is however now defunct, but as of the period it was still in use, it provided a blazing fast maximum connection speed that hit megabits per second. The various devices that support this Wi-Fi model are no longer being made; hence, today's devices would not support it.

IEEE 802.11a: This was created about 2 years after the original, and it worked on the 5GHz band. It was created, with the creators hoping that it brings about lesser interference. This was the school of thought when the version was created because most of the devices that interfered with the previous version ran on the 2.4GHz band. This is also as fast as the original; there was a record of the speed hitting 54Mbps. One thing this version of the Wi-Fi standard lacked was a range, as it was always having issues with devices on its path.

IEEE 802.11b: This was also created in 1999, but it was the version that made use of the 2.4GHz band, and it could reach a maximum speed of 11Mbps. It was this standard of the Wi-Fi that got the Wi-Fi technology popular.

IEEE 802.11g: This was designed in 2003, and it could attain a speed of 54Mbps while working on the 2.4 GHz band. After this, the standard was widely accepted, as it solved the issue of compatibility with several devices and offered high speed.

IEEE 802.11n: This version of the Wi-Fi was created in 2009, but it was not so widely used as its predecessors. It could operate on both the 2.4GHz and the 5 GHz bands. It also supported usage across different channels. One each channel, a speed of about 150Mbps can be achieved, hence, a cumulative of 600Mbps.

IEEE 802.11ac: This is the most current version on new devices. It was released in 2014, and with its technology, all devices connected to it can attain a speed of 1300mpbs. This is not the only feature on this update; it also has the MU-MIMO support, as well as additional Wi-Fi broadcast channels for the 5 GHz band. With a single router, this standard can support more antennas than the previous ones.

IEEE 802.11ax: This is the most recent standard. With this standard, the connection speed is possible up to the tune of 10Gbps. That's how far it can go, and works are on to make it go beyond. The capacity is also more than that of the ac, as it designed to add more broadcast sub-channels, and upgrade of the MU-MIMO, as well as allowing for simultaneous streams of data.

Over the years, Wi-Fi standards have only gotten better, and we are bound to see more. Connections on wireless networks are secured to get faster, and the advent of 5G will ensure this. 4G offered streams of data, more rapid than was experienced with the 3G, but 5G is going to be even faster and more reliable. The use of 5G transcends just connections to the internet; it's going to be the basic framework of wireless networking in the whole world, a total revolution of the way we have devices connected.

The various standards of Wi-Fi, especially the latest versions, have been compared to the Ethernet connections concerning speed. The 802.11n which can achieve a combined 600Mbps when compared to the

Ethernet speed of 100Mbps seems faster. However, it isn't just about the number; when it comes to real-life usage, the Ethernet connection is bound to outdo the 802.11n.

One thing is sure, though, development of the Wi-Fi is constant, and it follows closely as technology improves across the world.

Before we move on, did you wonder why the 100Mbps of the Ethernet connection will outdo the 600Mbps of the 802.11n? Well, this is because some factors limit Wi-Fi connections. These are; network protocol overhead, radio interference, physical obstruction between devices, and distance between the devices. All these problems are eliminated with the use of wired connections.

Also, when several devices join on the wireless connection, there is a decrease in performance. This decrease in performance results from limitations on the bandwidth and the hardware supporting the network.

These are the significant reasons why wireless networks still aren't as perfect as the wired connections. Of course, this is solely in terms of speed.

Wireless Interference

Do you have an idea of what wireless interference means? Just by the term, you already have an inkling into what it means, and with all that has been said so far in this book, you probably know what it can cause. However, there is a need to know all that causes wireless interference, to avoid them too.

Wireless interference is defined as a situation in which a Wi-Fi signal is disrupted as it travels through space. This is a crucial cause of inconsistent and unstable wireless connection in today's world. If all these can be eliminated, wireless connections would technically surpass wired connections. The problem is, how can they (the causes) be removed? They can't. The best way around this problem is to create a system that works well in spite of the obstructions.

There are various causes of the wireless interference, these are;

- **Building constructions**

With the advent of tall buildings, and other structures here are there, there is an increase in the interference being faced by wireless connections. The materials used in these construction result in interference, as they absorb or reflect the radio waves that the signal is comprised of.

For instance, if metals, concrete, and ceramics are used in a building's construction, they can degrade the waves that pass through them. Hence, it is best to get these out of the way, if the network is to remain optimal.

There are several cases in which spotting the cause of the interference is relatively hard to do. Do you know that lead paints used on the wall of some buildings can result in wireless interference? Yes, it can. However, it might be hard to identify or do anything to this. Irrespective of how thin or thick the layer of lead is, it can result in this interference.

- **Electronic devices**

Most of the electronic devices also have their radio waves. These waves are most often than not, in the same frequency as that of the wireless network from the routers and other access points. Being on the same frequency, there is bound to be interference between the two waves, and this is not good.

For instance, if you are in the kitchen, and your phone is connected to the home's router. When the microwave which also has its frequency is on, interference may occur. It is best to keep these two wave-emitting sources away from each other.

- **External factors**

Other external factors can result in interference. These include; construction or utility industries. In many other cases, power lines can also cause interference with Wi-Fi signals. Broadcast television or cameras can also cause interference.

On construction sites, overhead cranes or scaffolding are also known to result in wireless network interference.

It might sound funny, but trees that have broad leaves are also known to cause signal interference. This is because the water degrades the signal that the plant contains.

- **Range**

This is another factor that is considered to be a major cause of network interference. In this case, wireless network signals are doused as they travel a longer distance. The farther the signal travels, the weaker it becomes. This is as a result of attenuation. Attenuation is a process in which there is a reduction in signal strength throughout a travel.

Wi-Fi signals are known to travel better in the air than they do in solid materials, but with longer distances, they tend to lose their strength. By the time they get to the destination, there is bound to be interference. The only way to eliminate attenuation that results from a distance is to make sure the connected devices are always within just 30 meters of the signal source.

All these factors are confirmed to result in interference, as well as do many other factors. You can see that the probability of eliminating all these obstacles is very low. Hence, wireless network interference will only persist.

Data Security

This is another aspect of the wireless network that needs proper and critical consideration. Security is a big issue when it comes to wireless connections, and any enterprise ready to set up a wireless network should be prepared to invest so much in the security of data.

Data security as a concept refers to the various measure put in place to ensure that digital privacy is guaranteed, in the bid to restraining unauthorized access to computers, databases, and websites. These measures also function in the prevention of data from being corrupted. Irrespective of the organization's type or size, data security is critical.

Brief examples of the measure that can be taken in this light are; backup, data masking, and data erasure. One critical measure that is held in very high esteem is encryption. In the case of encryption, digital data, software/hardware, and other devices are encrypted. This measure renders the content therein on these devices and platforms unreadable to unauthorized users and hackers.

Another method of data security is authentication. This requires authorized users to provide a password, code, biometric data, or some other forms of data. These are needed in a bid to verify identity before accessing a secured system containing data.

These digital security measures are not only needed for enterprises and big companies. They are also of immense importance for health care records. Given this, health institutions are beefing up security and making their systems less vulnerable to intruders.

The importance of data security cannot be overemphasized. To an extent, every business needs it to stay ahead of the competition and keep profit margins high. Right from the banking sector that deals with volumes of personal and financial information, too small businesses that have contact details of customers at hand. You need security on your phone.

Don't you know why you need to secure your data on the phone? If you are one that makes use of Google Chrome, and you have all your passwords saved with Google's "Remember Password," you need it. Your Google account is probably logged in on your chrome to enjoy a more personalized browsing experience. In the settings page, all your saved passwords to the different websites are saved and can be easily viewed.

Hence, if a third party can quickly gain access to your phone, this data is at risk of being thrown to the public. The third-party might use these details to commit fraudulent activities in your name.

All data collected by an organization needs to be secured, and this is the primary purpose of data security. Whatever form of technology, or device that is used to store the information, it must be protected. Either it is a big firm or a micro-business, once there is a consumer data breach, it can lead to huge fines and litigation cases, just as big tech companies like Facebook and Google have been faced with in recent times. More than it was before, the security of data is now paramount, and big companies are investing so much into this.

Types of Data Security explained

There are various types of data security being used at different levels of data entry and output. The need for measures at different stages is to ensure that data breach becomes more difficult. Most often than not, the threat faced by companies is always of external sources. Here are some measures of securing data;

- **Data encryption:** This is a security measure in which code is being applied to every data string, causing access to the data to be restricted, until an authorized key is used.

- **Data masking:** This is another way from barring the third party from data. In this case, specific parts of data are masked; hence, both unauthorized external and internal parties cannot have access. Popular examples of data masking are where the first 12 digits of a credit card number are not displayed. Or when trying to recover Google account, the first 9 or 10 digits are not displayed, just so the system can be ascertained that the authorized user is the one trying to access the system.

- **Data erasure:** This is a data security measure employed when one has no use for particular data anymore. This measure causes the data to be erased from every system. An example is when you are trying to unsubscribe from a mailing list. By clicking the link, your detail is removed instantly and permanently from the list.

• **Data resilience:** This is a measure in which organizations create copies of particular data, such that when one copy is lost, it can be recovered from the cloned copy.

Compliance and Standards of Data Security

Platforms and organizations that collect data are known as data processors. This is an enormous responsibility for such an organization. There are different rules and regulations that guide how the data can be used. This regulation covers all data, irrespective of its type or size.

However, different industries field different regulations. The regulations in the tech industry are somewhat different from those in the finance industry. The rules sometimes are also influenced by location. For instance, companies dealing with citizens of the European Union might be faced with GDPR in the case where there is a data breach.

Fines are popular ways in which companies and enterprises that fall short of data breach regulations are punished.

Firewalls defined

The term firewall is one that flies around in the IT eco-space, and if you are entirely new to the system, you might wonder what it is, what it does, and how it works. Well, here it is.

Firewalls are network security devices that are designed to monitor both outgoing and incoming network traffic. It also doubles in functioning as a block and permission to data packets, with all its actions based on particular security rules.

The primary purpose of the firewall is to make sure that there is the presence of a barrier, right in between your internal network system and the external traffic of data coming from foreign network sources. For instance, if your company manages a LAN, any data that is to go into the LAN from another source will first have to go through the firewall. This way, vibrated and malicious data traffic can be identified and blocked.

How does the firewall work?

The working of the firewall is simple. It analyses the incoming traffic, comparing them to some set of pre-established rules imputed into it, and blocks every data that does not meet up to the instructions. The firewalls are always situated at the port, which is the network's entry point. It is at the ports that information is exchanged with external devices. An example of this is

"Source address 172.18.1.1 is permitted to reach 172.18.2.1 via port 22."

Any confusion? Here is another analogy. Think of your IP address as a house, and the port numbers are the rooms in the house. The house (destination) can only be accessed by trusted persons (source address). After this, there is further filtering that only allows specific persons to enter particular rooms in the house. The rooms in this case are the destination ports. It all depends on what type of data is coming in. Some data can access any of the ports, while others can only be allowed through one.

Types of firewall

Now that you know what firewalls are all about, it then begs the question "how many types are there?" There are different types of firewalls out there. They can be software or hardware. It all depends on what you want in your organization. The best bet is to have both system functional in your enterprise.

With the software firewall, there is its installation on every computer linked on the network. On installation, it regulates every traffic through port numbers and applications. For the physical firewall, there is the installation of a device in between the network and the gateway.

The packet-filtering firewalls are divided into two main categories, which are; stateful and stateless. The stateless firewalls are those that cross-check the packets exclusively from other packets, and there is no context in this check. This way, they can quickly identify hackers and other vices. For the stateful firewalls, they remember information about other packets that have been examined and are marked as safe.

These two types of firewalls are somewhat useful; however, they merely provide essential protection and have limitations. One such limitation is that they are unable to determine if the content of the request that is incoming will have an adverse effect on the destination application. In the case where a virus is coming in from a trusted source, these firewall types will never know.

The good news, however, is that there are advanced firewalls that will never miss such.

• **Next-generation firewalls (NGFW):** These are firewalls that are a combination of both traditional firewall technology and some other functions like encrypted traffic inspection, intrusion prevention systems, anti-virus, and many more. One primary function that is found in the next-generation firewall is the "deep packet inspection" (DPI). The essential firewalls discussed earlier will only search through the packets' headers, these go beyond to inspect the data contained in the packet. This enables users to easily identify, categorize, and obstruct packets that are virulent.

• **Proxy firewalls:** This functions by filtering network traffic at the application level. However, unlike the necessary firewalls, it acts as an intermediary between two end systems. In this case, there must be a request from the client to the firewall. This request is then evaluated and compared against set security instruction. The result of this cross-check determines if the packet is blocked or allowed.

In most cases, the proxy firewalls are employed to monitor traffic for layer 7 protocols such as HTTP and FTP. This system of firewall also makes use of both the deep pocket inspection and the stateful inspection;

- **Network address translation firewalls (NAT):** This allows several devices that have independent network addresses to communicate and connect to the internet while making use of just one IP address. This way, the individual IP address of the computers are hidden. Due to this, hackers can't capture specific details of a particular computer. This is a step further at ensuring the security of systems on a network.

The NAT firewalls have close similarities to the proxy firewalls. They are somewhat an intermediary between a network of computer and outside traffic.

- **Stateful multilayer inspection (SMLI) firewalls:** This firewall system is designed to conduct the filtration of packets at the network, transport, and application layers. At the filtration stage, it compares them with trusted packets before a decision is being made. Just like the NGFW firewalls, these conduct examination of the whole packet at every layer, before either passing or blocking them.

This search aims to determine the state of the communication that is being proposed, such that only a connection with trusted sources is allowed.

Wireless networks are the future, and there is so much to do in ensuring that they are effective and make communication occur in real-time. With data packages of digital entities such as games, movies, audios, etc. improving an achieving better resolutions and quality, it is only right that the supporting systems follow suit.

Making sure that wireless networks can attain uninterrupted transfer of data like the wired connection is still a long drive from being achieved. This, coupled with the need for security, are the problems being faced by the wireless network. Research, innovation, and system developments are continually underway to ensure improvement, and we can only be sure of more shortly.

Chapter 4: Revolutionary Impact of the Wireless Technology and Breakthroughs of Computer Networking

Since the advent of wireless technologies, decades ago, our lives have never remained the same. And one thing is sure; it only promises to be better. With the gradual evolution of 5G in the mainstream, we can only imagine what is to come. One sentence does it, "Wireless technology has affected the very intrinsic properties of our lives."

It has affected the way we do business; it has transformed the way we learn; it has affected the way we communicate and keep up with family and friends. Everything has changed, and this is just a testimonial of things to come.

Over the course of the several decades in which we have had wireless technologies, there have been several breakthroughs. A whole book can be written to discuss strides that have birthed revolutionary platforms and infrastructure that have made life easier today.

For the sake of brevity, two of these important breakthroughs will be discussed in this chapter. These are; VLAN and the Internet.

VLAN – Virtual Local Area Network

The VLAN is also known as the Virtual Local Area Network, and from the name, you can tell that it is bound to have similar frameworks to the LAN. The concept of VLAN is also simple. It is a sub-network that can group collections of devices, done on a separate physical LAN. You understand what a LAN is, right?

What the VLAN does as against the LAN is that it makes it very easy for an administrator to partition a single switched network to match the functional and security requirements of their systems. This is achieved without the need to run cables or make some significant changes to the whole infrastructure of their network. This system of computer networking is always done by more significant enterprises in a bid to re-partition devices for better management of traffic.

The use of VLAN in organizations is very important because they can cause an improvement in the overall performance of a computer network, as devices are all grouped based on the frequency of communication between them.

With the VLAN, there is also the provision of security on more extensive networks, as there is an allowance of a higher degree of control over which devices can communicate with one another. VLAN is very flexible, and this is achieved because of logical connections, unlike the LAN and WAN that are physical.

There is the possibility of several independent VLAN to be supported by network switches. This goes on to create the second (2) layer (data link) of the implementations of the subnet. Broadcast domains are always associated with the VLAN, which most time is comprised of several network switches.

Types of VLANs

There are several types of VLANs, which include; protocol-based, static, and dynamic VLANs.

- **Protocol VLAN** – This type of VLAN handles its traffic based on the protocols that have been programmed into it. In this system, there is a switch with the function of segregating and forwarding traffic based on the various traffic protocols.

- **Static VLAN** – this type of VLAN is also referred to as the port-based VLAN. This system needs a network administrator with the function of assigning ports on a particular network to a specific virtual network

- **Dynamic VLAN** – In this system of the VLAN network, there is a network administrator with the sole function of defining membership based on the characteristics of the devices. This is unlike the switch port location.

How does VLAN work?

The working of the VLAN is simple, so also is its function. The ports situated on switches are capable of being assigned to a VLAN or more than one. This enables the division of different systems into logical groups. This division is based on which department the devices are associated with. When the division is done, there is then the establishment of rules about how the systems that are located in the various groups can communicate with each other.

Different types of groups can be formed, ranging from practical and straightforward groups to the more complex and legal groups.

Then, there is the provision of a data link access by the VLAN, to all hosts connected to switch ports that have been programmed by the same VLAN.

There is an entity called the VLAN tag, which is a 12-bit field in the Ethernet header. It is designed to provide support for up to 4,096 VLANs per domain switch. This tagging by the VLAN is regulated and standardized by the IEEE (Institute of Electrical and Electronics Engineers) 802.1Q, which is most times referred to as Dot1Q.

At the reception of the untagged frame from the attached host, the VLAN ID tag that has been configured on that particular interface is then programmed to the data link frame header. 802 1Q formats achieve this programming or configuration. After this, the 802.1Q frame is then passed to the destination.

Each of the switches, in this case, makes use of the tag to keep each traffic by a VLAN in a separate lane from the others. Hence, the passage is only to the specific location where the VLAN is configured. The tags are what is used to ensure this distinction. When the frame is finally at its switch port destination, there is a removal of the VLAN tag, before transmission of the frame to the end device.

It is possible to configure several VLANs on a particular port, with the use of the trunk configuration. In this case, each frame is sent via the port, with a VLAN ID, just as it has been described above. Another device interface that wants to receive and transmit tagged frames must be able to support the trunk mode configuration. When there is an Ethernet frame that remains untagged, there is a default VLAN for it, which most likely will be defined in the switch configuration.

At the reception of an untagged Ethernet by the VLAN switch, the VLAN tag is assigned to the ingress interface. The frame is subsequently forwarded to the port of the host that has the MAC address. The MAC address is the Media Access Control Address.

In the case of Broadcast, unicast and multicast, they are all passed towards all ports that are located on the VLAN. In the case where there is a reply from an unknown host to a hidden unicast frame, there is an automatic learning of the location by the switches. Hence, subsequent frames that are addressed to that host are not flooded.

The switch-forwarding tables are updated by two different mechanisms. The very first is that the old forwarding entries are removed from the forwarding tables from time to time. The interval at which this removal is done can also be configured prior. The second mechanism is that, whenever there is topology change, it causes a reduction in the forwarding table refresh timer, and refresh is triggered. By this reduction in the timer that has been configured, the time refreshes earlier.

There is the Spanning Tree Protocol (STP) which is used in the creation of loop-free topology among the switches in each layer 2 domain. You can always make use of a per-VLAN STP that causes different layer – topologies to reduce STP overhead, whenever it is the same topology with the multiple VLANs. With the STP, there is the blockage of links forwarding which has the potential to produce forwarding loops — thereby creating a sparring tree from a particular root switch.

Thanks to this blockage, some links will not be used for forwarding. They have to wait till there is a failure on another part of the network which causes STP to make the link a part of an active forwarding path.

Advantages and Disadvantages of the VLAN

The benefits of the VLAN include security, a reduction in the traffic from broadcast, easy administration, and the confining of the broadcast domain.

On the downside, there is a limitation of 4096 VLANs on one switching domain, which creates several issues for hosting providers.

The communication of data between the several VLAN fostered by a router. However, some modern switches also feature router functionalities; hence, they are called layer 3 switches.

The Internet and how it has impacted our lives

The whole of the internet is a vast concept that has defined the very intrinsic parts of our lives. The world is at a stage referred to as the information age, and the very core of this is the internet. The internet is a vast planet of connected devices on which communication, information, and connectivity are fostered.

The internet is global network of computer networks, which are now based on wireless communications, ultimately providing a ubiquitous capacity of multimodal, interaction that is not limited by distance. Right there from where you are, you can access information and reach out to anyone, in any other part of the world, and this is done in real-time. There is no loss of time, and there is no lag, once your internet connection does not lag. This, is one way in which technology has revolutionized our lives.

Don't be surprised to know that before the internet, there is something called the Arpanet. This was first deployed in the year 1969. As of this time, it was controlled by the U.S Department of Commerce. This control by the government limited the adaptability of the platform. It was when the platform was finally privatized in the 1990s that it eventually became widely accepted and used across the world.

As of 1996, a survey of internet users counted at about 40 million, and in 2013, the number of internet users has risen to 2.5 billion persons. Of this number, china has the most significant amount of internet users.

In the earlier days, the speed of accessing the internet was minimal, due to the mode of connection required. However, with the explosion of the wireless connection, internet speed has become amazingly faster. And with 5G underway, it can only be faster.

The central concept of the internet is the ability of it to production, distribution, and use of digital data and information in whatever format they may come.

The effect of the internet on our way of life is beyond words; the closest is to say it has brought about a revolution. A revolution in every aspect. As coined by

Ithiel de Sola Pool in 1973, the internet is just the technology of freedom.

Three factors contributed majorly to the growth of the internet.

• The developer of the World Wide Web, Tim Berners-Lee, was ready and willing to share the source code of his technology to the global community, to foster its development caused the major boom. He also shared the TCP/IP internet protocols of the technology, and till today, about 2/3 of the internet is operated by an open-source server called Apache.

• There was also an institutional change in how the internet is being managed, as it was taken from the government, and can be managed by the global community of users. By privatizing the internet, it can then be used for both commercial and cooperative uses.

• There was also a significant shift in social structure, culture, and social behavior. Networking became a prevalent organizational form

These factors combined to birth the evolution we have today as the World Wide Web. This is the most significant breakthrough in technology in the 20th century, and it has opened a whole new world to the global community. The internet is now facilitating Businesses, education, culture, finance, entertainment, and many other aspects of life.

Social Media on the Internet

The internet opened the door for many other innovations, with innovators coming up with majestic ways to make use of the internet. This brought a whole new way of making money. Various structures and infrastructures popped up rapidly on the internet. This period of rapid development is referred to as the dotcom bubble.

After the dotcom bubble and in the early 21st century, there was the birthing of a whole new world. A world where the very natural way of life of humans – the social aspect, can be fostered. Humans are social animals, and with dotcom innovations, this aspect was brought online.

The very first in this line was the creation of Friendster in 2002. This brought about a social-technical revolution, and in no time, several platforms that allowed for real-time interaction and communication amongst people.

In the earlier stage of communication on the internet, mails were the order of the day. However, social network sites have transcended what the emails could offer. Now, we have fully established companies in this stream of innovation; Facebook, Instagram, WhatsApp, Twitter, Tiktok, Etc.

New Media (Mass Communication)

With the advent of the internet, we have had a new form of media referred to as the New Media. New media is a term that is used in the description of the content that is produced by the use of several forms of electronic communications, aided by computer technology.

New media is premised on the idea of interaction, and this is made possible by the internet. Basked in the concept of new media, we have websites, online video/audio, streams, emails, online social platforms, online forums, online communities, blogs, web advertisement, etc.

This new form of media might not easily be separated from the old media, with the only distinction being that the internet serves as an outlet for the new media.

Chapter 5: Wireless Network Computer Architecture

Wireless network is a whole broad concept that has revolutionized the way we do things. It has totally caused an overhaul over the whole connection of computers. Earlier in this book, we have seen the various components used to foster the wired networks. Similar components are also needed for the wireless networks. Of the overall computer network infrastructure in the world, the wireless networks contribute only to a portion. Irrespective of how limited this infrastructure is, attention is needed to ensure that functionality is ensured.

In this chapter, we will be taking a close look at the various components of the wireless communication. Will also consider the wireless application protocol, its models and its architecture. Further, we will delve into the architecture of Bluetooth, MOBITEX, CDPD and I-MODE. Read on.

Components of Wireless Communication

Wireless communication has become an intrinsic part of the way we relate with other humans. This is thanks to the rapid development and significant innovations over the past few decades. A world where there is no need for wires to aid the transmission of data from one point to another.

Wireless communication has made the exchange of data and information as easy as it can get. There are the various types which include; radio broadcast, infrared, satellite, microwave and Bluetooth. Some of these will be discussed in the following chapter.

Here are the components that make up the basic infrastructure of the wireless communication network;

- **Users**

This is the most vital part of the wireless communication network. This factor does not necessarily mean a human entity. Users simply mean any entity that makes use of the wireless network, directly. Of course, the most common types of users are people. But as said earlier, being a user is not limited to this scope. The user can also be a robot, which receives an instruction over a wireless network, right from a central computer which controls a manufacturing process. Basically, the wireless network is to serve the user, hence, the main beneficiary of the wireless network is the user. This makes them really critical in the scope of things on the wireless network.

The user has the ability to initiate and terminate the use of a wireless network, hence it is safe to also refer to users as "end-users." Whoever operate the computer that is designed to perform a variety of application specific tasks, with the wireless network being the interface, is a user.

Users of a computer network can either be static or mobile. The ability to make use of the wireless networks on the move is one reason why they are so popular. This is a limitation on the part of the wired network. It is very possible for an individual to make use of the school Wi-Fi while moving through the campus.

There is also the case in which a computer is operated over a wireless network for an indefinite period of time. This might take place in an office or a location with faster internet connection

- **The Computer Devices**

This is another important component of the wireless network. This are referred to as the clients, existing upon the wireless network. On a wireless network, there are different computers devices based on the function they perform on the network. There are some that are basically for the end-users, while there are others that are end systems. Computer devices are able to communicate with each other over the same wireless network.

The various end systems on a wireless networks are servers, databases and websites. These end systems are containers with a repository of information that can be viewed end-users in different locations. On the part of the users, any device can be adapted and used in accessing the information desired. For instance, a user can buy and install a wireless network interface card (NIC) within his laptop. When this installation is done, he is able to operate on a particular type of wireless network.

The various computer devices always have an operating system that differentiate them. There are different operating systems (OS), which include; windows, LINUX and the Mac OS. The main function of the operating system is to drive the software that is utilized in the realization of the network applications.

- **NICs**

This is known as the Network Interface card and it has been discussed earlier in the course of this book. It is a very important part of the wireless network, just as it is on the wired network. These devices are mainly plugged into the computer system, however, in some cases, they can also remain as an external device.

- **Air Medium**

Air or better still, the atmosphere has a function that transcends just the sustenance of life. Over the past decades, it has served as the medium that cultivates the propagation of the wireless communications signals. This propagation is the major factor of wireless networking. It foster the transmission of information across computers and other ends on the wireless network.

Information and data on the wireless are conducted via, hence, they are subject to the various limiting factors discussed earlier. The quality of transmission is always dependent on obstruction in the air and the range over which the signal is to travel.

Wireless Application Protocol

The Wireless Application Protocol is a specification designed especially for a category of communication protocols, which is used in the standardization of how wireless devices are used in accessing the internet. The devices in this case are mobile phones and radio transceivers.

Internet access is a ubiquitous functionality, which is achieved with the use of different technologies. The idea of the wireless application network was conceived by four companies, namely; Ericsson, Motorola, Nokia and Unwired Planet.

There are four main layers of the Wireless Application Networks, which are

- **Wireless Application Environment (WAE):** This is the application layer, which contains device specifications and content development programming languages like WML.
- **Wireless Session Protocol (WSP):** This represents the session layer, which causes a provision of fast connection, suspension and reconnection.

- **Wireless Transport Layer Security (WTLS):** This is the security layer which provides the system with data integrity, privacy and authentication.

- **Wireless Transport Layer (WTP):** The transactional layer which runs on the User Datagram Protocol. One of the main function is that it offers transactional support.

- **Wireless Datagram Protocol:** This is the transport layer which represents consistent data format.

WAP Model

The WAP model is very simple. It involves a user opening the browser on a mobile device. He types in the URL of the website he would like to visit in the browser. The URL is encoded and then sent to the network with the help of the WAP protocol via the WAP gateway.

As the data reaches the WAP gateway, the request is then translated to a conventional HTTP URL request, which is subsequently sent over the internet. When the request finally gets to the destination web server, it is processed and a response is sent back to the device via the WAP gateway. The response is sent in form of a WML file which can only be viewed by a micro-browser.

WAP Architecture

The peculiar factor about the WAP model is that there is the presence of different layers. These layers are arranged in a peculiar architecture which fosters the actualization of task designed for it. Basically, WAP is designed in a layered fashion. As a result of the layers, it can be very extensible, as well as being flexible. One other factor that makes the WAP framework special is that it can be scalable. In the paragraphs above, we took a cursory look at the various layers

These layers are the very basis on which WAP runs.

Bluetooth Architecture

The term Bluetooth is probably not new to you, it shouldn't be. With the use of mobile phones and personal computers, Bluetooth has been ubiquitous as it is one of the earliest form of file sharing over the wireless network. With the aid of Bluetooth, there is no need for a USB cable to transfer files. A simple tap and connect will do the trick. However, we aren't going to discuss the various functions of the Bluetooth or what you can do with it.

The Bluetooth is a wireless connection concept that many remain in the dark of. The Bluetooth framework consist of both the hardware aspect and the software aspect. In fact, Bluetooth is a hardware-based radio system, just as it is a software stack which specifies a link between the two architectural layers.

The main thing about the Bluetooth architecture is the protocol stack. It is the protocol stack that really defines the working of the Bluetooth. This stack, just like the WAP is a set of layered programs. Each of the layer communicates with the layers above and beneath it.

This is it, one stack of Bluetooth protocol has two layers in it. The main layers are the lower level hardware radio system and the upper level software stack. It is the upper level software stack that specifies the linkage between the two layers.

Lower Stack Layers

This is the basics of the functionality of the Bluetooth framework. The basic layer is referred to the radio layer, which can also be called the module. This layer describes the physical features of the transceiver. The main function of this layer is the transmission and reception of radio frequencies over the 2,4Ghz band. This is what is referred to as the physical wireless connection. This functions by splitting the band of transmission into 79 different channels, ultimately providing for fast frequency hopping. This is done for security.

Right in top of this layer, there is the baseband and link controller protocol.

Don't get confused, the baseband has the function of the proper formatting of data, which is subsequently of data to and from the radio. It is what brings about the definition of the timing, framing, packets and the flow control that exists on the link.

The link manager then brings about the translation of the host controller interface (HCI) command, from the level of the upper stack, then fosters a connection which it thereafter maintains.

Upper stack layer

This layer of the Bluetooth framework is focused on the build of devices that are designed to communicate with one another, by leveraging on the core technology.

The interface between the software and hardware of the system is the Host controller interface.

There is then the Logical link control and adaptation protocol which is just a level above the HCI in the upper stack. The main function of this protocol is the fostering of a communication between the two layers of the Bluetooth stack. It also performs the function of monitoring the source and destination of data packets. This is the most critical part of the Bluetooth framework.

Just above the logical link control and adaptation protocol layer, the protocol stack is not linearly ordered. However, there is a protocol layer referred to as the service discovery protocol, which has an independent existence. It performs the function of interfacing between the link controller as well as bringing about an interoperability between two Bluetooth end devices.

MOBITEX

Have you ever heard of the term MOBITEX and wondered what it meant? Well, if you are an enthusiast, you should have found out more about what the term means. Just as we have the WAP and Bluetooth architecture, there is also the MOBITEX architecture. It is a wireless network architecture that fosters a framework for the fixed gadget needed run wireless terminals in a packet-switched, radio-based communication system.

The MOBITEX framework has three major components. These are; radio base station, the MX switch and the network management center (NCC). This framework was first developed in 1984 by Eritel, which was a subsidiary of Ericsson.

The radio base station has the function of transmitting for each single cells up to a distance of 30km. the base stations go on to carve out a coverage area, as well as determining the network capacity. This is the basis of the communication over mobile phones. Your phone gets connected to the nearest MOBITEX source to you, and there is no problem of connection when you change location.

This technology is less expensive than the circuit-switching technology. The MOBITEX packets have a limitation of 512 bytes of data. Each packet that is transmitted contains information of its source as well as destination.

Efficiency in the use of the packet-switching technology comes from the fact that the packets can be transported in any direction and in any order. When all the packets then get to the destination, the packets are rearranged into the right order.

The MX switches are another component of the MOBITEX framework. This mainly controls the communication routes to and from the base solutions. It also controls the communication between wireless and fixed devices. The various switches can be rearranged in hierarchy, into groups according to regions and areas.

CDPD

This is shorthand for Cellular Digital Packet Data, and it is a specification that is used in the support of wireless connection to the internet as well as other public packet-switched networks. The various mobile phones and modem that offer the CDPD support bring about internet connection to a speed of 19.2kbps. The CDPD is an open specification which strictly adheres to the framework of the Open System Interconnection model. This utility is also able to extend in the future.

CDPD as a framework can offer support for the following; internet's protocol, ISO connectionless Network Protocol and IP multicast service. With the multicast framework, a broadcast of updates can be fostered to the sales and service section of an organization. This framework can also be used in the transmission of updates to recipients on a news subscription service.

In the case of mobile users, a persistent link can be avoided since there is CDPD's support for packet-switching. This way, a particular broadcast channel can be used by different users at the same time. When the connection is made, the modem of a user is able to decipher and accept the packet meant for it. For instance, when there is an email coming in, it is directed immediately towards the user without the need for a circuit connection.

The CDPD architecture exists simultaneously with the AMPS network, which makes it able to support both data and vocal communication.

Features of the CDPD technology

- The communication established between the base station and the M-ES is a full duplex
- Its framework makes use of the 30KHz channel by current AMPS/GSM networks, with which it is able to transmit data at a rate of 19.2kbps
- It makes use of the same frequency used by AMPS
- It also makes use of the DSMA technique
- This framework offers support for numerous services and can connect to the backbone of the internet.

The CDPD architecture

There are three main interfaces on the CDPD network, which are the E-interface, I-interface and the A-interface. Basically, the E-interface is known to exist between the CDPD and the fixed network on the outside of the CDPD. While the I-interface is known to exist between one CDPD network and another CDPD network. For the A-interface, it fosters a connection between the BS and MS. The A-interface can also be called the Air Interface.

There are different elements used in the CDPD architecture

- **M-ES:** The function of the M-ES is also similar to that of the subscriber or mobile unit that any cellular system makes use of. For the M-ES to function, there is the need for a SIM that can be contained in a laptop, mobile or PDA. It has a function of serving as the interface between radio equipment at a rate of 19.2kbps. The various M-ES has its own unique NEI (Network Equipment Identifier), which is associated with its home MD-IS.

- **MDBS:** The function of this element is similar to that of the Base Station. It performs a main function of broadcasting available channels for the M-ES. This element also manages various radio activities which include channel allocation, usage, etc.

- **MD-IS:** The main function of this element is to foster a connection between the internet and PSDN. It can also function as a frame relay switch and a packet router. The buffering of the various packets is achieved by the M-ES. With this element, there is also the support for roaming management, because it contains registration directory.

Advantages and Disadvantages of CDPD

There are some pros and cons to the use of CDPD.

Pros

• The very first advantage is that it can make use of existing channels that are on the AMPS network. This makes it very easy to install and use.

• The architecture is like that of the cellular, which causes it to support larger capacity. It can offer this much support because it can be easily upgraded.

• Also, when there is the need to establish a data call, there is no lag. The lag is eliminated because the CDPD phone is already registered on the CDPD network.

Cons

• For the CDPD network, there is no mesh connection. Due to this, there is a lack of a direct communication between two M-ES.

• Also, there is a limitation on the CDPD cell size to about 10 miles.

I-MODE

Have you ever heard of what is referred to as the I-MODE. It was somewhat of a miniature internet, operated right out of Japan. The service was offered by DoCoMo, and it can be easily accessed directly via a menu on the I-Mode-Compatible devices. It makes use of the DoCoMo packet-switched technology, and this brings about an 'always on' network access. Billing on subscribers is always based on the amount of data sent and received, unlike other frameworks that may bill based on time spent in accessing the service.

Understanding the I-Mode technology is very pertinent. That it is not common again does not mean it is difficult. For web developers, HTML is all that is needed to upload it. All that is required for compatibility is some little changes to the webpage. This causes it to fit to the screen of the mobiles.

One of the changes that is needed is that the security and bold frames on the websites should be removed. In propagating the framework, DoCoMo made a partnered venture with web developers to create and information oriented site into the I-Mode form.

The I-Mode framework functions by sending information in the form of small packets, which delivers top-notch services to clients.

Chapter 6: Wireless Communication Technologies

If there is anything the wireless technology has achieved for us, it is effectiveness in communication. Without the need for wired connections, you can reach out to anyone, anywhere they are in the world. Wireless communication is a form of wireless networking which makes use of similar components as discussed earlier in this book.

With all that has been discussed so far, you should have a deep insight into what wireless networking and communication is all about. As simply put, wireless communication is a system of data communication which is executed and delivered without a wired connection. This term in itself is a very broad one. It involves all the procedures and types of connection that can be fostered between two or more devices via wireless signals.

Basic components of the wireless communication systems

There are three basic components of the wireless communication systems. These elements are the; transmitters, the channel and the receiver. These are the basic building blocks of the wireless communication systems.

- **Transmission path**

The transmission path of the wireless communication system is comprised of the encoder, encryption, and modulation and multiplexing. Whenever there is a signal from the source, it is transmitted through a source encoder. This then converts the signal into a suitable form that can be used in various signal processing techniques.

When the encoding is done, whichever information is left is subsequently removed, resulting in an optimal resource utilization. The signal resulting from the encoding is then subjected to an encryption standard. This encryption causes the information and its signal to remain protected and secured from unauthorized personnel.

One of the very popular encoding techniques to use is the channel encoding. This causes the signal to suffer from reduced noise impairments and interference. When the channel encoding is being carried out, a level of redundancy is introduced to the signal. This causes the signal to be robust against noise. There is then the subsequent modulation of the signal with a suitable modulation technique.

When all these are done, the signal can be easily transmitted over an antenna. Subsequent to modulation, multiplexing is carried out. There are various multiplexing techniques, which are; Time Division Multiplexing (TDM), Frequency Division Multiplexing

(FDM). Multiplexing is important, as it leads to the sharing of a valuable bandwidth.

- **Channel**

Talking about channels, these refer to the medium of transmission used in wireless communication. One very important fact to note about the channel is that it is very unpredictable and the details can change any minute. This makes it somewhat being defined as unstable. It is prone to interference, distortion, noise, and scattering. All these ultimately lead to a received signal that is filled with errors.

- **The Reception path**

The primary function of the receiver is the collection of signals from the channel, which is then decoded to form the source signal. This part of the wireless communication system is made up of demultiplexing, demodulation, channel decoding, decryption and source decoding. The reception path has a framework that makes it just function inversely to the transmitter.

When there is an incoming signal from the channel, it is received by the demultiplexer, which goes on to separate it from other signals. Thereafter, there is the demodulation of the individual signals, hence recovering the original signal. The channel then functions to eliminate redundant signals.

With decryption, the signals' security is removed and then interpreted as a simple sequence of bits. There is then the transmission of the signal to the source decoder which recovers the original transmitted message.

Types of Wireless Communication Systems

The use of mobile phones has necessitated the need for various services to be made available on the go. These services include calls, internet access, multimedia and other utilities that are now featured on today's mobile phones. Thanks to the wireless communication systems in place, all these can be performed in real time.

There are various wireless communications systems out there, however, here are the most commonly adopted;

- **Television and radio broadcasting**

If you are conversant with your history books, you should understand that the radio is the first form of wireless communication that was executed. The radio broadcasting is a form of Simplex communication system. In this system, there is the transmission of information just in one direction, and there is the reception of the same data by all users.

- **Satellite communication**

This is arguably one of the most important form of wireless communication we have in the world today. With this form of wireless communication, there is a worldwide network connection without it being hindered by population density. This wireless communication system offers telecommunication, positioning and navigation, broadcasting, internet, etc. Basically everything we need on our smartphones are tied to this. Beyond mobile communication, modern television broadcasting and radio systems are all dependent on the satellite communication systems.

- **Mobile telephone communication system**

When it comes to the mobile phone technology, this is the most used communication system. With the advent of this technology, there has been a radical transformation of the way we do things in the world. The activities that can be performed on the mobile phone transcends just making calls, but to features like Bluetooth connections, Wi-Fi, GPS, FM radio.

- **Global positioning system (GPS)**

This is somewhat a subcategory of the satellite communication systems. This system provides users with services ranging from navigation, to positioning, location and even speed. This services are made possible by the GPS receivers and data from the satellite.

- **Bluetooth**

This is another low range wireless communication system. The Bluetooth framework is able to provide data, voice and audio transmission. The transmission range of Bluetooth is about 10 meters. Basically every computer device (including mobiles) are fitted with this technology. Though there has been the innovation of faster alternatives, it still remains widely used. Phones, tablets, computers, etc. are all fitted with the technology.

- **Paging**

Do you remember pagers? Yeah, that obsolete mode of communication. By the way, are there still people that carry pagers around? I doubt it. The paging technology however was a major success back then. This was before mobile phones took over the mainstream. This technology functions by relaying information in the form of messages. It is also a simplex system.

- **Wireless Local Area Network**

We have discussed the WLAN earlier in this book. It is also a form of wireless communication technology. With the aid of the WLAN< devices can connect to other access points and the internet.

- **Infrared communication**

This technology was somewhat used in the mobile phones earlier in the century, however, its usage is now limited to remote controls for televisions, cars and audio equipment. It makes use of infrared waves of the electromagnetic spectrum.

Multiple Access Techniques

Before we delve in the various multiple access techniques there are, a quick look at what multiple access means, is pertinent. Multiple access is a technique which allows several users to share allotted spectrum in a very effective manner. Due to the limitation of the spectrum, there is the need to share, which would ultimately improve capacity. This process is executed by allowing for the use of available bandwidth by several users at the same time.

With respect to computer networking and communications, the multiple access allows different terminals to one multi-point transmission medium. Hence, there is transmission and sharing over this network.

Frequency Division Multiple Access (FDMA)

This is the segment of the frequency band that is allotted for wireless cellular telephone communication in 30 different channels. Each of these channels conveys a voice conversation. The FDMA is a fundamental technology employed in the analog advanced mobile phone service (AMPS). The AMPS is the most installed form of cellular phone in North America.

The very basis of the FDMA is that a particular channel is only assigned to one user at a time. This is the framework used in the Total Access Communication System (TACS). On the Digital-Advanced Mobile Phone Service, there is also the use of the FDMA. However, in this case, there is the addition of time division multiple access. This results in three channels for each of the FDMA channels. Ultimately, this results in the tripling of the number of calls that can be handled on the channel.

Time division multiple access (TDMA)

The Time Division Multiple access technology is sort of a complex one. This is because it needs a level of synchronization to exist between the transmitter and the receiver. This technology is widely used in the digital mobile radio system.

This digital cellular telephone communication technology brings about sharing of a particular frequency without the advent of interference. The basic functioning of this framework is that it divides a particular signal into various timeslots, thereby enhancing the data carrying capacity.

The various mobile stations assigns a frequency for the exclusive use of a time interval. In many cases, the total system bandwidth for a period is not assigned to a station. But the frequency of the system is subdivided into what is referred as sub-bands. When this is done, TDMA is then used for multiple access in each of the sub-bands.

There are several advantages to the use of TDMA. It gives room for very flexible rates. Also, it can withstand gutsy and variable bit of traffic. There is no guard band needed for the wideband system.

There are however some downsides to the TDMA. It has a high data rate of broadband systems, which need some complex level of equalization.

Code division multiple-access (CDMA)

This is another form of multiplexing which brings about different signals occupying a particular transmission channel. The CDMA brings about an optimization of the available bandwidth. This technology is used mainly in the ultra-high frequency cellular telephone systems.

This multiplexing technique differs from that of time and frequency multiplexing. In this case, as a user, you have access to the whole bandwidth for the whole time. This system has a basic principle which involves the fact that it codes to distinguish one user from the other.

This allows for use by users that might count up to about 61, all at the same time. Calls and theoretical limits are differentiated by the 64 Walsh codes. The maximum number of calls is reduced by factors like operational units and quality issues.

There are four factors that actually affects the capacity of the CDMA.

- Processing gain
- Signal to noise ratio
- Voice activity factors
- Frequency reuse efficiency

On CDMA, users are on different frequencies which are separated by code. This means that CDMA can always function effectively in the presence of noise and interference.

Advantages of CDMA

- The CDMA framework requires a very tight control on power. This means that, when a user is close to the base station that is transmitting with the same power, the signal will drown. To prevent this, the power on the signals must be higher or lower than that of the receiver.

- The signal reception can be improved by rake receivers.

- In the case of the CDMA, flexible transfer may be used.

- The CDMA framework is designed to reduce interference

Disadvantage of the CDMA

- The length of the code must be carefully selected to avoid complications.

- For proper functionality, time must be properly synchronized

- Due to the gradual transfer, there is an increase in the use of radio resources, which ultimately reduces the capacity of the signal.

Space division multiple access (SDMA)

This is a satellite communication system which leads to the optimization of the radio spectrum usage and also minimizes system cost by taking advantage of the directional properties of dish antennas. The Space Division multiple access is also known as Spatial division multiplex. The satellite dish in this framework has the function of transmitting signals to different places on the earth.

One fact that you should note is that, for the SDMA framework, you need to carefully choose the zone for every transmitter. Also, there is the need for a precise antenna alignment. If there is every any error, it can lead to the failure of one or more channels. Also, it leads to interference among the various channels.

Spread spectrum multiple access (SSMA)

For the spread multiple access, signals are being used once they have a transmission bandwidth which has a magnitude that is greater than the minimum RF bandwidth required. There are two main types of the spread spectrum, which are;

• **Frequency happed spread spectrum:** In this digital multiple access system, the carrier frequencies of the individual users vary in a false fashion within the scope of the wideband channel. In this case, the digital data is split into similarly sized bursts which are subsequently transmitted on several other carrier frequencies.

- **Direct sequence spread spectrum:** Of the SSMA types, this is most used for the CDMA. In this case, each of the users have their code word which is orthogonal to the codes of other users. Whenever there is a need to detect the user, the receiver must know the code that is being used by the transmitter.

Channel Characteristics

There are several characteristics of the wireless communication channels. The important characteristics are;

- **Path loss:** This can be expressed as the ratio of the power of the transmitted signals with respect to the power of the same signal being transmitted by the receiver, on a particular path. This factor is a function of the propagation distance. In designing and deploying wireless communication networks, there is the pertinent need to estimate path loss.

Also, there are a number of factors that influence path loss, examples are; the radio frequency used as well as the nature of the terrain.

- **Fading:** This is another characteristic of channels. This phenomenon refers to a fluctuation in the signal strength when it gets to the receiver. There are two main types of fading, which are;

- Fast fading (also known as small scale fading)
- Slow fading (large scale fading)

Fast fading is the case in which there is a drastic fluctuation in the phase, amplitude and multipath delays of the received signal. This is due to the interference between several versions of similar transmitted signals that arrive the receiver at different periods.

There is another factor referred to as delay spread. This refers to the period between reception of the first version of the signal and the last echoed signal. There are three propagation mechanisms that result in fading, these are; reflection, diffraction and scattering.

Slow fading is as descriptive as it can get. This implies signals that fades away very slowly. There are features that characterize slow fading. It is a form of fade that occurs when there is the absorption of transmission between the transmitter and receiver. This phenomenon is referred to as slow fade because it takes a couple of seconds or minutes for its completion.

- **Interference:** Every wireless connection has the tendency of suffering from interference. There are several sources from which this can emanate, but they are categorized in two; adjacent channel interference and co-channel interference.

In the case of adjacent channel interference, signals in nearby frequencies have components not in their local environment. These component therefore have the tendency of on-going transmission being interfered by adjacent frequencies. This interference can however be avoided by the introduction of guard hands situated between the stipulated frequency ranges.

The co-channel interference in some cases is being referred to as narrow band interference. This interference form is always due to nearby systems that resonate on a closely similar transmission frequency.

- **Doppler shift:** This is another factor that affects wireless communication. This occurs as a result of the fading generated in the signal. Doppler shift occurs whenever there is movement by the transmitter, relative to the receiver. This movement relative to the receiver causes a change in the frequency of the signal. Hence, there is a different in the frequency of the signal at the transmitter and the receiver. This phenomenon can be easily observed in sound waves.

A practical way of observing this is in an incoming car. The sound coming from the car becomes louder as it approaches you, and grows thinner as it speeds past you and away.

Types of Paths

In the transmission of signals from the transmitter to the receiver, there are two main types of path that can be followed. These are; direct-path and multi-path. The path followed somewhat influences the extent to which the wireless channel characteristics affect the transmitted signal.

Direct-path: There is no twist to the definition of the direct path. When the transmitted signal reaches the receiver directly, it is said to have passed through the direct path. There are some components involved in this transmission, and they are called the direct path components.

Multi path: In this case, the signal from the transmitter reaches the receiver having passed through different directions. By passing through different directions, the signal is subjected to different phenomenon. This transmission is enabled by different components referred to as the multi path components.

The various phenomenon that these signals are exposed to includes; reflection, diffraction and scattering. When they finally reach the receiver, there is an alteration in the amplitude, frequency and phase. This is unlike what will be achieved with the direct path.

Diversity and its types

There are different receiver techniques, of which Diversity is a powerful one. Diversity as a communication receiver technique makes provision for link improvement at a relatively low cost. The main function of the various diversity techniques is to result in an overall performance of a fading radio channel.

In this system, the receiver is provided with several copies of a particular information. These signals are then transmitted over two or more real/virtual communication channels. Owing to this, it is safe to conclude that the basic concept behind diversity s repetition or redundancy of information.

Types of diversity

There are different types of diversity, which are;

• **Frequency diversity:** This is a form of diversity in which the same informational signal gets transmitted on several carriers. In this case, the frequency separation between the signals is a minimum of the coherence bandwidth.

• **Time diversity:** This is a form of diversity in which the informational signal is transmitted in sequential intervals. In this case, there should be a greater transmit times tan the coherence time. The time interval in this case is solely dependent on the fading rate, and this increases with a decrease in the fading rate.

• **Polarization diversity:** In the case of the polarization diversity, the electromagnetic field of the signal bearing the information is modified. This leads to an orthogonal type of polarization.

• **Angle diversity:** In the case of the angle diversity, the directional antennas are used in the creation of independent copies of the signal being transmitted, and this is done over multiple paths.

- **Space diversity:** Space diversity involves several antennas receiving information at different locations they have been placed. This causes different signals to be received independently.

Diversity is a very important aspect of transmission. In most of the cases in which diversity is employed, it is the receivers that makes the diversity decisions not the transmitter.

Chapter 7: Wireless Technology for Internet of Things

Communication technologies across the world has become as easy as it can get. Right from wherever you are in the world, you can reach out to anywhere. Thanks to wireless networking, interconnectivity between various devices is possible and can be done in real time. Communication has transcended what it used to be many years ago. Now, we are in the world that has seen devices interacting with themselves, and with humans.

Internet of things is gradually becoming s pivotal topic of interest in the technological world. It's not only going to influence the way we live our lives, it's also going to influence the way we work. You surely must have heard my people herald what you need to know about working in the future. While all these is true, you should know that the future is here already. Computers are connected with each other in very easy fashion, unlike anything that has been seen before. There are technicalities surrounding IoT, but they are all understandable.

Internet of Things simply involves the connection of any device with an "on" and "off" switch to the internet or with another device. Just about any device you can think of can enjoy this connection. Talk of your coffee maker, washing machines, headphones and even lamps. It is called Internet of Things because it is a gigantic connection of things. This relationship can be fostered between people – people, people – things and things – things.

Internet of things is a broad concept, in which wireless communication plays a major role. At the very heart of everything related to internet of things is wireless communication. It is this technologies that allow for communication between devices. There is a communication fostered without the devices having to be connected to each other. The mode of connection is mostly the radio frequency or RF. This communication framework is not entirely new, as it has been around since the early 20th century. Rather than becoming obsolete like some technologies of the 20th century, it has grown and evolved to meet every day needs of the 21st century.

Later in this book, we will take a deeper look into internet of things and what the future holds for it. However, in this chapter, we will take a look at the various wireless communication technologies that have been instrumental in the development of internet of things, over the years.

Zigbee Wireless Technology: Its Architecture and application

There are different wireless technology out there, but one can easily dismiss the Zigbee wireless technology as the most excellent. This is because it is low-cost and low-power consuming. It also has a number of great characteristics that makes it just excellent. It is the best suited technology for embedded applications, industrial control, home automation, etc.

The main function of the Zigbee wireless technology is to power controls and sensor networks. This is achieved o the IEEE 802.15.4 standards for wireless personal area networks (WPANs). This is a form of communication standard that defines both physical and media access control layers. This is done so that it can handle devices at low-data rates. The various Zigbee WPANs are able to function at 868 MHz, 902 – 928 MHz and 2.4 GHz frequencies.

This wireless communication technology is used to control and monitor applications, all within the range of 10 – 100 meters. This form of communication comes at a cheaper cost, and simpler than the others like Bluetooth and Wi-Fi.

Zigbee is able to offer support for different network configurations, and it can be operated in different modes since the battery is conserved. The Zigbee networks are designed to support extension of use with routers. It can also allow for many nodes to be interconnected with each other. This way, a wider area network is built.

The Zigbee Architecture

The system structure of Zigbee consists of three different devices, which are the Zigbee coordinators, router and the end device. In every Zigbee network, there must be the presence of at least one Zigbee coordinator. This coordinator acts as the root and bridge of the network. It is also responsible for the handling and storing of information whenever there is the reception and transmission of data over the network.

The routers in this case act as the intermediate that moderates the passage of data to and fro a device to another. For end devices, they have a limited functionality which is just to communicate with the parent nodes.

In the Zigbee wireless communication network, the number of coordination, router or end device involved is always dependent on the type of network being established. There are different network types, which are star, tree and mesh.

In the Zigbee wireless communication architecture, there are different layers.

• **Physical layer:** This layer is responsible for modulation and demodulation whenever there is a transmission and reception of signals on the network.

• **MAC (Medium access) layer:** This layer is one which takes the responsibility of reliably transmitting data by gaining access to several network on the Carrier Sense Multiple Access Collision Avoidance (CSMA). The MAC layer is also responsible for the transmission of beacon frames for synchronization communication.

- **Network layer:** The network layer is the one responsible for all network related operations like network setup, routing, end device connection and disconnection to network.

- **Application Support Sub-layer:** The application layer is one which enables the various services that are necessary for interfacing between the Zigbee device object and application objects and network layers for the purpose of data management. The application layer support sub layer is responsible for the merging of devices based on specified services and needs.

- **Application framework:** The framework layer has two data service types which act as the key value pair and the generic message services.

Zigbee Operating Modes and its Topologies

There are two modes with which data on Zigbee can be transferred, these are the non-beacon mode and the beacon mode. In the case of the beacon mode, both the coordinators and routers are designed to continuously monitor the state of the data coming into the system. Whenever the Zigbee system is in this mode, the routers and coordinators are always in a state of activity. This is because there can be an awakening of the node for communication, at any point in time.

In the beacon mode, there is no communication of data from the end devices, when this happens the routers and the coordinators are forced into a sleep state. From time to time, the coordinators get active and transmits the beacon in the direction of the network's router. The beacon networks are known to work in situations where there is a need for communication in lower duty cycles and longer battery usage.

The beacon and non-beacon types of the Zigbee networks helps in the management of periodic, intermittent and repetitive data types.

There are three main topologies on the Zigbee network, which are; star, mesh and cluster tree topologies. All of these topologies are known to always contain one or more coordinator. In the star topology, the Zigbee network consists of one coordinator. This coordinator is responsible for the initiation and management of the various devices situated on the network.

Devices that communicate directly with the coordinator are known as the end-devices. The star topology is a system employed in a network where all the end devices are needed to communicate with the central controller. The high point about the star topology is that it is very easy to assemble and deploy.

In the case of the mesh and tree topologies, there is the extension of the Zigbee network with numerous routers, and the coordinator is needed to star them. With the adjoining of these devices, there is communication with other adjacent nodes to enable the provision of redundancy to the data. If there is ever a failure of a particular node, other devices on the network receives this information, thanks to the topologies structure.

Mesh topology is used mainly in industries because there is so much importance placed on redundancy.

Specifically for the cluster-tree network, every cluster is made of a coordinator and several leaf nodes. The coordinators in turn are connected to a parent coordinator that serves as the initiator of the entire network.

Application of Zigbee Technology

- **Industrial automation:** This is one major way in which the Zigbee network is utilized. It reduces communication cost and it also optimizes the control process, making it more reliable.

- **Home automation:** It is also perfectly adapted for use in the control of home appliance, such as light control, appliance control, and control for heating and cooling systems as well as other security appliances in the home.

- **Smart Metering:** The Zigbee remote operation can be used in smart metering such as energy consumption response, pricing support, etc.

- **Smart Grid Monitoring:** Zigbee network can also be used in the operation of smart grid systems.

WiMax

WiMax is acronym for Worldwide Interoperability for Microwave Access. It is the technology standard that is employed in long-range wireless networking. The use of WiMax is effective for both mobile and fixed connections. However, in recent times, the use of WiMax has declined, despite being envisioned to be a leading form of internet communication and the widely adopted alternative to cable and DSL.

One factor that has inhibited it wide adoption is the high cost. The technology is not a replacement to Wi-Fi, neither is it a replacement for the hotspot technology. But if faced with the need to install either of a standard wired hardware as with DSL or the WiMax, the latter is cheaper.

There are two basic forms of the WiMax, which are base stations and the receivers. The base stations are installed by service providers used in deploying technology in a particular area. While the receiver is the part of the network installed by the client.

Advantages of WiMax

The network framework is very popular because it comes at a lower cost. It is also very flexible in nature. When compared with other internet technologies, the WiMax can be installed faster. The installation time is always lower because all that is needed are short towers and lesser amount of cable.

With the WiMax, you can also enjoy voice and video-transferring capacity, alongside telephone access. In the areas where it is not economical to execute wired technologies, WiMax is the best option.

Disadvantages of WiMax

With the WiMax, connection strength reduces as the user pulls away from the source. Also, WiMax has suffered a decline in popularity, which has caused many mobile devices not to have built-in WiMax support.

Advantages of Wireless Technology

Changing right from wired technologies to wireless technologies is just as pertinent as it can get for your organization. It is one big step that your facility needs to take, and there are many reasons for this. Compared to wired network technologies, wireless technologies have some benefits that give them an edge.

- **Increased Mobility**

This is one of the revolutionary advantage that has revolutionized our lives. Now you can get connected to others devices or the internet, right from anywhere you are in the world. With the advent of mobile technology, mobile users are granted access to information in real-time. Also, if you work for a corporate organization, you can access your company's network, without being stuck at a particular location. This way, teamwork and productivity is improved, which is near impossible on wired networks.

- **Installation speed and simplicity**

With the use of the wireless systems, there is a reduction in the amount of cable needed. Wired networks are always cumbersome to install and setup. Also, the setup of wired networks can prone safety issues, especially post installation. Also, installation of the wireless network is as fast as it can get.

- **It offer wider network reach**

If there are places in your organization that cannot be reached by wires, the wireless network comes in handy. Wireless connections can extend to just about anywhere you want it to get.

- **It is more flexible**

There are always upgrade in technology, and your communication systems are boud to suffer from the need for upgrade. If your organization makes use of the wired communication network, it may be cumbersome to upgrade. However, with the wireless technologies, you can easily upgrade your communication system. Update to meet new configurations are very easy to achieve on the wireless network.

- **Reduced ownership cost over time**

Well, setting up a wireless network at first may be costly, than the wired network. However, overtime, you will find out that it actually costs you lower. Other than the fact that it will stand the test of time, it will also save you the stress of always laying new wires and hardware when there is the need for upgrade.

- **Increased scalability**

You can always configure the wireless networks to meet some application's specific requirements. You can easily enact changes and scale to this process whenever the need be.

Disadvantages of Wireless Technology

Despite the fact that with wireless technologies, you can allow different users to access a large repository of information with the hassle of running wires, there are some downsides to its use.

- **Cost**

This is one critical factor that puts off people with the use of wireless network. They are typically expensive to install and setup. Though this is the only time you need to spend much. At setup, you might incur a cost four time more than you would with the wired network.

- **Coverage**

There is always a limit on the range that can be covered by the wireless network. For example, a router has just a range between 150 to 300 feet.

- **Dependability**

This is another issue with the wireless network, it is very prone to interference. It can be easily interfered by radio signals on similar frequencies, as well as radiations from other devices. Physical structures can also be a source of interference.

- **Security**

The wireless network has the issue of security, as it can be easily accessed by any computer within the range of the network. Once information is being transmitted by network, it can be easily hacked into, even if the information is encrypted.

- **Speed**

Without mincing word, it is known fact that the wireless networks are somewhat slower than the wired networks. In some cases, it reaches up to 10 times slower.

Top Wireless Technology Challenges

Though the wireless technology has taken our lives by a storm, basically every connection can now be done wirelessly. However, the technology is yet to make the use of wires obsolete. There are a number of challenges that are faced by the wireless technology.

- **Physical Connectivity**

In a study on some volunteers, it is identified that one of the major challenges faced by the use of wireless technology is physical construction of components. There is always a limitation on the wireless networks. In areas such as basements, lower floors and in buildings made of steel, there is always the deflection of network signals. There are many cases in which terrain has been the issue. In many of the cases studied, participants need to first install a distributed antenna system, or a mobile virtual private network before they enjoy enhanced network.

- **Technology Connectivity Issues**

Bandwidth needs to be further improved if the wireless network is going to support large streams of data at once. There are innovations bound to solve this actually, especially with the 5G network. However, until its overall adoption all over the world, it remains a major issue that needs to be tackled.

- **Security**

Security is still a big issue with the use of wireless networks. Just as there are tools and frameworks integrated to protect the wireless networks, they are still subject to cyber-attacks. Though by-passing a system's security is not an easy nut to crack, people still find their way around it. Security is yet to be total on the wireless network. Once the network can be accessed or visible in a particular location, it can be bridged. This fact opens organizations with the wireless networks to incessantly upgrade their security frameworks and all. There is the need to employ an IT security expert to monitor and maintain the security protocols that keep the system safe and reliable.

- **Management**

There are several times that system get down times. To ensure that users have the best experience, management is saddled with the responsible of being aware of issues ahead of the users – in real time. Hence, there is a need to constantly execute surveys and tests on the network to upgrade and maintain the system.

Chapter 8: Network Protocols

Protocols are intrinsic properties of what makes computer systems function effectively. They are like dictators or map with which the system follows to carry out specific tasks. Without the protocols, it may be hard to execute anything with the computer. Technically, a protocol can be defined as a set of rules on which communication is based. Protocols are agreed set of guidelines, which makes things work.

Different aspects of wireless communications have specified protocols adapted for them. In this chapter, we will be taking a deeper look into the various protocols we have.

Internet Protocols

Internet protocols are set of digital messages formats and rules that are needed for the proper exchange of messages between computers across a single network or a group of network connected to one another. This system of instructions make use of what is known as the internet protocol suite, which in most cases is referred to as TCP/IP. The exchange of this messages between the computer and the network is done in the form of datagrams (also known as data packets).

The most primary of the internet layer of the internet protocol suite is the IP. The IP is a set consisting of several communications protocols, which are made up of four abstraction layers. These layers are; link layer, internet layer, transport layer and the application layer.

The IP has a primary function, which is the delivery of the datagrams from the source to the designated host. This transport is directed by the address on the packets. The IP system has a specific method with which addresses are labelled on (within) the datagrams. This process is referred to as encapsulation.

Types of internet protocols

What do you think the internet is? Many people make the mistake of thinking that the internet is the common World Wide Web (WWW). WWW is just one part of the vast internet that is made up of other components like the FTP, Gopher, Telnet, etc.

There are several protocols used on the internet, each of which has its own standard and usage.

- **Electronic mail**

As a statement of fact, there are three protocols that facilitate each email you receive. These are the Simple Mail Transfer Protocol (SMTP), Internet Message Access Protocol (IMAP) and the Post office Protocol 3 (POP3).

For the SMTP, it is a protocol used in the transfer of mail away from a mail box, while the latter two are needed for the reception of the mail. Virtually every internet service provider have a framework that support these three protocols.

• File transfer protocol

This is shortened as the FTP, and this is the protocol in play when you transfer files from one computer to another. This is also commonly used when you uploading a web page to a server, to make it visible on the World Wide Web. To use the FTP, you need a special program known as the client.

• HTTP (World Wide Web)

This is referred to as Hypertext Transfer Protocol. It is the protocol in use by web servers, which makes it possible for web pages to be visible in a web browser. For every web address you want to visit, when you look in the address bar, you will see the prefix http://. This information is mostly on display and in the web address bar because some browsers are capable of enabling FTP. This way, it gives the browser a heads up on what type of information to expect.

• News (Usenet)

Network News transfer Protocol is one used to facilitate UseNet. This is similar to the forums that are situated on web pages. On the UseNet, there are also forums that are specially meant for companies with a range of topics. UseNet can be used in various niches, ranging from computer related topics, science, discussion, etc.

- **Gopher**

This is another tool used on the internet. There is every possibility that you aren't aware of a protocol as this. It functions primarily in the enabling of a browser to search for information, without knowing the location of the material. You are able to search for a list of information, then culminates them and send to you.

- **Telnet**

This is a protocol that allows you to operate a particular remote computer right from anywhere you are in the world. You can operate the computer, just as though you were sitting right in front of it. Once you are logged in, you can control your remote computer that is far away from you.

Transmission Control Protocol (TCP)

This is one of the most important wireless communication protocols. It is also basically used for the transfer of data over networks. This protocol set works just perfectly with the Internet Protocol (IP), and the duo is referred to as TCP/IP. While the IP part of the network is meant to address and forward data packets from the source to its destination, the TCP takes control of ensuring reliability of the transmission.

What does the TCP do?

As said, the TCP is meant to ensure that transfer of data is as reliable as it can get. On the internet, transfer of data is done through packets. Packets are data units sent independent of each other on the network. Once these packets reach their destination, they are arranged and reassembled.

Data transmission on a particular network is done in layers, and each of the layers carry out functions that are complementary to that of the others. The TCP and IP are designed to work hand-in-hand in each layered stack of information.

TCP is bothered with the control of transmitted data, while IP takes care of the channeling on the network. And in the case where there is the presence of Wi-Fi, it controls the transmission on the local area network.

You should be familiar with the basic function of the TCP by now, which is "it is responsible for ensuring reliability in the course of transmission." There are some factors which determine how reliable a transmission is. A reliable transmission

• Is one in which no packet is lost in transit i.e. they all get to their destination.
• Is one in which every delay that affect data quality is eliminated

- Is one in which there is the orderly reassembling of all data packets.

How TCP works

During any transmission, all packets are labelled (numbered) by the TCP. Other than the numbering, TCP also allocates deadline at which all packets must have reached their destination. Whenever there is the reception of any packet, the source device is notified by a packet known as acknowledgement.

When the deadline is passed, and there is no acknowledgment received at the source, it sends another copy of the packets. With this done, you can be sure of the orderly rearrangement of the packets.

TCP Addressing

Unlike the IP, there is no elaborate addressing system on the TCP. For the IP, it is referred to as the IP addresses. The main fact is that, TCP does not need to have one. In the TCP framework, it only makes use of numbers that have been provided by the device it is working on, for identification of source and recipient packets.

The labelling numbers are referred to as ports. For instance, on the web browsers, port 80 is used for TCP. Emails make use of port 25. This port number if also used alongside the IP address, so we can have something like "192.168.66.5.80."

User Datagram Protocol (UDP)

Don't get lost with the several protocols there are, you may not need all of them throughout your career. In fact, most of them are as automatic as they can get, just doing their thing. Another important protocol is the User Datagram Protocol (UDP). The UDP is the simplest transport layer communication protocol that you will ever find on the TCP/IP protocol suite.

It is called the simplest by no mistake, as it comprises of a minimum amount of communication components and mechanisms. In some cases, the UDP is known to be unreliable. However, it makes use of IP services, which sort of optimizes its performance.

One glaring shortcoming of the UDP framework is that the receiver does not create acknowledgments for package received, unlike the TCP. In fact, the sender does not wait for one. This is a really big gap that the framework fails to fill.

Requirements of UDP

You may wonder why we need to use this framework in wireless communication, when there are other reliable alternatives. Well, the UDP is mainly used in cases where there the various acknowledgment packets use similar bandwidth with the original data being sent. For instance, you can use UDP while streaming videos, as any lost packet will not be noticed.

What are the features of the UDP?

- This framework is mainly used in cases where there is no need for acknowledgment of data
- Also, in the case where data only goes in one direction, UDP comes handy
- It is very simple and adapted for communications based on Query
- It is not connection oriented
- There is no provision of congestion control mechanism
- Delivered data may end up not being ordered
- It is stateless
- It is best adapted for use in streaming applications like the VoIP.

UDP Header

There are four main parameters of the UDP header.

- **Source port:** this is the 16bits information on the UDP whose function is the identification of the packet's source
- **Destination port:** This is also a 16 bits information with the function of identifying application level service at the particular destination
- **Length:** This is a specification of the whole length of the UDP packet.

- **Checksum:** This is the parameter that serves as storage for the value of checksum generated at the packet's source before transmission.

Applications of UDP

There are several areas where UDP is used in the transmission of data, and these are;

- Domain Name Services
- Simple Network Management Protocol
- Trivial File Transfer Protocol
- Routing informational protocol
- Kerberos

The systems in which UDP is used in data transfer are however not limited to these.

Wireless Network Protocols

In most cases, wireless networks are mistaken to be Wi-Fi networks. But as established earlier in this book, Wi-Fi is different from wireless communication technology. Wireless network protocols are proven to be of immense use in consumer devices.

LTE

The LTE technology has a design which enhances data rates as well as other problems experienced in old phone protocols, such as roaming problems. On this protocol, rate reaches up to about 100 Mbps. However good this technology may be, there is still a limitation as the phone carriers are not deployed in some areas. This lack of phone carriers is due to high cost of installation and government regulations.

LTE technology however is not designed to support home and LAN networks, but designed to support consumers in longer distances.

Wi-Fi

We have discussed the whole concept of Wi-Fi earlier in this book. Well, the technology has become the default connection technology employed in homes, offices and other personal areas. The technology became popular in the late 1990s. There are cases in which the technology can be controlled to travel over longer distance. But in most cases, they are best suited for more personal and home use.

WI-Fi actually has the protected access security protocols which adds a level of authentication to the network, as well as data encryption. This access technology is mainly to prevent third party from having access to the network or mining personal data.

Bluetooth

This is one of the most popular wireless technology in the world. It was created in the 1990s and it i=has risen to become ubiquitous. Unlike the Wi-Fi, just a minimal amount of power is needed to run the Bluetooth effectively. Hence, Bluetooth is designed to only travel shorter distances when compared to the Wi-Fi. In many equipment, Bluetooth has been replaced by WI-Fi.

60 GHz Protocols – WirelessHD and WiGig

Video streaming has become a very popular activity to engage in on the personal computer. This has necessitated a wireless network protocol that can better support it. These were created in the 2000s to offer high definition streams.

Wireless Home Automation Protocols – Z – Wave and Zigbee

These are wireless protocols designed for home automation. They are designed to make use of low energy consumption.

Network Routing Protocols

Ever heard something called the routing protocol, and you just wonder what that is? It's pretty simple. A routing protocol makes use of software and some routing algorithms to determine the best mode of transfer of data and information between nodes. The main functions of the routing protocols are to create a router communication, as well as an overall network topology understanding. In some cases, the routing protocol is also referred to as the routing policy.

In a bid to foster a more effective communication between computers, the routing protocols have been developed and innovated over time. The working of the routing protocol is pretty simple.

- **Discovery:** The process of identifying other routers situated on the network
- **Route management:** Keep tabs on the various potential destination on a network
- **Path determination:** This is the process in which the protocol makes a decision on where it should send the network message.

There are some routing protocols that give a full details of mapping of the network links, while others just allow routers to work with lesser information.

Classes of Routing Protocols

There are 3 major classes of routing protocols

Distance Vector routing protocol

These protocols are designed to help choose the best paths (in the basis of hop counts) needed to reach a destination on particular network, in a particular direction. Some of the protocols in this class are dynamic, which makes them optimal for the performance of the function. One of such is RIP. In this framework, the hop counts are the various routers that exist between a source and the destination network. Of all the various possible paths, the one with the least hop count is decided to be the best path.

Features

- The network update are exchanged periodically
- The updates are always broadcast
- The routers in this framework make decisions premised on information from neighboring routers.

Disadvantages

- The periodic exchange of information most times result in an unnecessary traffic
- The exchange also results in security issues
- The broadcast of network periodically most often than not will create unneeded traffic.

Link State Routing Protocols

Unlike the other protocol, these routing protocols know more about the internetwork. These are also known as SPF (shortest path first). An example of this is OSPF.

Features

- The updates in this protocol can only be initiated when there is a change in topology.

\- Only that much updates are exchanged which is requested by the neighbor router.

There are three tables that this routing protocol maintains, which are;

\- **Neighbor table:** This is the table that serves as a repository of information about the neighbors of the router only.

\- **Topology table:** This is the table with the information about the whole topology, which include both the best and back up routes that information packet can take.

\- **Routing table:** This is the array of the best routes on the network.

Advanced distance vector routing protocol

This is somewhat of a hybrid, a culmination of both the link and vector routing protocols. One example of routing protocol in this class is the Enhanced Interior Gateway Routing Protocol.

Types of Network routing protocols

As explained above, all the routing protocols are classified into three. There are several routing protocols that makes the wireless and wired networks function effectively. These are;

Routing information protocol

This is the routing network that is extensively used in both local and wide area networks. It is shortened as RIP, and its functioning is premised on the distance vector algorithm. The protocol has been defined since 1988, and has since then had two versions. You can use any of the versions nowadays.

Interior gateway routing protocol

This routing protocol is one made by CISCO, and it is used in routers to exchange routing data within an independent system.

Open shortest path first

This is an active routing protocol that is used in internet protocol. It is an example of the link state routing protocol and it includes all the major group of interior gateway protocols. This protocol is mainly used in companies with a big network.

Exterior gateway protocol

This is the ultimate routing protocol for the internet, and it was specified in 1982 by Eric C. EGP. It was initially expressed in RFC827, but properly specified in RFC 904 in the year 1984. The topology on this network routing protocol is like a tree.

Enhanced interior gateway routing protocol

This is another type of the distance vector routing protocol, but it is fitted with advanced technology to reduce the unsteadiness that occurs whenever there is a change in topology. It enjoy a general optimization based on DUAL work, as well as a loop free operation. This network protocol also offers a means of speedy junction.

Order Gateway Protocol

These are the core network routing protocols found on the internet and is responsible for the maintenance of a table of internet protocol that are designed to allow network reaching capabilities within AS.

Intermediate system to intermediate system

This is a great protocol that is used by network devices to decide the best route to promote datagram, from one end to another of a packet on a switched network. This process is what is referred to as routing.

Network Security Protocols

The network security protocols are a type of network protocols that make sure that data and information being transferred over a network are kept safe and secure. These define the processes and methodology needed in securing network data from any illegal attacks.

These protocols are simply designed to make sure that data sent and received via the internet is kept safe and away from the prying eyes of illegitimate users. Hacking and other cyber-crimes are at an all-time high. Hence, you want to be really conscious of your security.

- **HTTPS:** This is the protocol used in protection of internet traffic. Anyone not on the traffic cannot access information that is transmitted via HTTPS.

- **Firewall:** This is a popular security protocol on networks. This protocol is extensively used in the E-commerce sector, to protect components which include Internet Payment Gateway, Server based Wallets and payment servers. If these are ever compromised, several users will be affected financially.

There are three main categories of the firewall;
- Packet filter
- Filter circuit level
- Application-layer filters

Packet filters are saddled with the responsibility of passing data that pass through a network interface. The information needed at this point is; IP-address, port numbers and destination. You can easily install and implement this firewall on your wireless network. The high side is that, it can be easily maintained. However, it offers a very low protection level.

The filter circuit is the intermediate level of firewall security. This is designed to monitor agreement activities at the junction of the client and external host, checking if the requested session is valid. This firewall type is not so expensive and is best used to protect private networks. However, it does not filter packets.

The application level filters provides your network with the highest level of firewall protection you can think of. However, it is a more complex design and comes at extra cost.

- **IPSEC:** This is a security protocol designed to encrypt data at the level of the network. There are three main protocols embedded in this; authentication header, encapsulating secure payload (ESP) and the internet key exchange (IKE).

The authentication header is responsible for providing data origin authentication, data integrity and security from repetitive messages.

The ESP is designed to offer validation and integrity for the payload, but it does not do so for the IP header.

For the IKE protocol, its main function is to solve the problems of key distribution protocols.

Other than the three main protocols running within the IPSEC framework, there are also two main configurations. The very first configuration bears the network layer protocol. While there is also the second configuration which is used for closing data within the network.

- **PCT:** This is shorthand for the Private Communication Technology, and it has a basic working process like the SSL. The only difference between the PCT and the SSL is the size of the message in transit.

Compared to the SSL, the messages on PCT are smaller. Browsers like the Microsoft Explorer 3 makes use of PCT. Unlike the SSL however, the PCT has more options in the negotiation of an algorithm and data formats.

Network Management Protocols

The names spells it all out. Network management protocols are suites of protocols that take charge of the definition of processes, and policies that manage, monitor and maintain a computer network. This set of instructions are known to convey and manage the various operations and communications that take place on a particular computer network.

In every management protocol, there is always the proposition of architectures and procedures needed to extract, collect, transfer, store and report information related to management. If you are looking to understand any management protocol, make sure you understand the architecture. This is really important.

Types of the Network Management Protocols

In this section of the book, we take a look at three of the most popular protocols you really need to know. There are others, but they comes at a reduced relevance, relative to these;

- **ICMP**

This is a network layer protocol which is a concrete part of the group of sub-protocols that are associated with the IP protocol. The main function of this protocol is the validation of faults, and also the ensuring of performance. It detects errors and send information back in that light. This is why the main messages y ICMP are error messages and control messages.

This is the protocol used in the calculation of factors like latency, response time or packet loss, etc.

- **SNMP**

This is the Simple Network Management Protocol, which is the application layer that oversees failures, performance and actions. The framework of SNMP is to gather, organize and communicate management information on the various devices situated on the network. This protocol is used in quite a number of hardware components, to ensure diversity of devices and also diversity of marks.

SNMP Architecture

There are two basic components of the SNMP framework, which are the SNMP agents and the SNMP administrators.

The SNMP agents are a bunch of software that run everything related to the elements that needs to be managed. They primarily collect data on the device

SNMP administrators are more involved in the management and monitoring section of the network. They serve as the centralized location for all data sent and stored.

How are data organized in SNMP?

Data that are in for management on the SNMP are known as objects.

OIDs (Object identifier): These are basic elements with the primary function of identifying objects. The OIDs are always in the format: .1.3.6.1.4.1.9.9.276.1.1.1.1.11. The extraction of this number comes from the system of hierarchical organization that starts by identifying the producer of the object.

MIBs (Management Information base) are the basic format that data from the SNMP agents to the SNMP managers follow.

- WMI

This is the Windows Management Instrumentation. This is mainly used in systems and devices that run on the Windows software. On the WMI framework, there is the model that represents, obtain and share management information on any hardware that runs on windows.

The Architecture

There are three fundamental entities on the WMI architecture, which are the WMI providers, WMI infrastructure and the administration applications.

The providers is in-charge of getting any management information from one object or the other.

The infrastructure is the framework designed to bridge the gap between suppliers and the management tools.

Protocols are what make things work on any computer network. It sort of the order and rules that guide every operation. If there are no protocols handling the various aspects of what goes on in a network, you can only imagine the amount of disarray.

Chapter 9: Communication and Cellular Systems

Communication in recent years is made possible by the cellular systems. Cellular communication is one that has been fostered by the use of Mobile phones. Our phones as we know them, are all based on cellular networks. Cellular communication is premised on the ability of radio to execute simultaneous transmission and reception. Mainly, on the cellular networks, there are geographical divisions of cells within particular cells.

The cellular has revolutionized the way we socialize as humans. This technology is constantly evolving, offering faster, effective and real-time communication in different forms.

Features of Cellular Network systems

The advent of the wireless cellular networks has served as a solution to the spectral congestion problem. And it has also increased the capacity of users. There are some features that make these possible.

- In a limited spectrum, there is the offering a high capacity
- It allows for the reuse of radio channels in different cells

- On the cellular network, there is the enabling of a fixed number of channels to serve a somewhat large number of channels. This is achieved by reusing the channels across different regions

- In this case, the communication always occurs between the mobile and the base station

- There is the assignment of neighboring cells to different channel groups

- The cellular networks ensure that interference levels are tolerable

- There is the presence of frequency reuse or planning

- There is also the organization of wireless cellular network

The Cellular networks are always organized into multiple low power transmitters.

Shape of Cells

The area covered by cellular networks are always divided into what is referred to as Cells. On each cell, there is the presence of antenna used for transmission of signal. One each cell, there are unique frequencies. Communication of data across cellular networks is always served by the transmitter at the base station, as well as the receiver and the control unit.

There are two main shapes of cells, which can either be squared or hexagonal

Square

In the square cells, there are four neighbors at a distance of "d," and there are other four at another distance "2d"

Hexagonal

This shape is recommended for use in most cases because it offers easy coverage. Another reason why it is recommended is thanks to the shape. There are some advantages that come with its use;

- There is the provision of equidistant antennas
- The distance from the center to the vertex is the same as the length of the side.

Frequency Reuse

This is a phenomenon in which you make use of the same radio frequency within a given area, especially when they are separated by a considerable distance, offering minimal interference in the bid of establishing communications.

There are some benefits from the concept of frequency reuse

- It fosters the communication within a particular cell on a particular frequency
- There is a limitation on the escaping power to the adjacent cells

- Frequencies can always be reused on close cells
- You can use the same frequency for more than one communication
- It is possible to have about 10 to 50 frequencies on a particular cell

Evolution of cellular networks

It all started with 1G, and now we are looking at a world connected by the supersonic 5G. How far and well has communication come over the past decades? The very first generation mobile network was introduced in the early 1980s. But with the explosion of users across the world, there is the need to always continue on the expansion of the communication networks.

It all started with the Italian inventor, in person of Marconi. He had succeeded in the transmission of Morse code signals with the use of radio waves. This went over a distance of 3.2kms. This was as far back as 1985. This was the very first wireless communication debuted in the world. Ever since, there has been a continued research into making radio waves better. Thanks to this invention, scientists and engineers began the development of compatible phones, as against the wired telephones that were in vogue.

The first generation mobile phone was invented by Martin Cooper, who was as of the time working with Motorola. The prototype was to be used in a car, and was developed in 1974. This invention is considered to be the turning point of communication in the world.

1G

This is the very first mobile network that greeted the world of wireless communication. This network hit the mainstream in Japan by Nippon Telephone and Telegraph Company, in 1979. In the 1980s, the use became popular in the US, Finland, UK and Europe. Analogue systems were used in this case.

Features of 1G

- It had a frequency of 800MHz and 900MHz
- It has a bandwidth of 10Mhz
- It made use of analogue switching technology
- It featured frequency modulation
- It makes use of a voice only mode of service
- The access technique is the frequency division multiple access

Disadvantages

- Due to interference, there was poor voice quality
- The battery life was very poor
- The mobile phone had large size
- It featured less security
- There was limitation on the number of users and cell coverage
- Roaming on the 1G network was not possible

2G – The Second Generation Communication System

The advent of 2G marked the start of the new digital technology. It was also referred to as the Global system for mobile communication. GSM technology soon became the standard for the development of the wireless communication. It was able to support up to 14.4 to 64kbps data rate. This enabled SMS and email services on mobile devices.

Features of 2G

- It supported SMS services
- It made roaming possible
- There is enhanced security on the network
- There is encrypted voice transmission
- It supported internet, though at a lower data rate

Disadvantages of 2G

- The data rate is very low
- There is a limitation in mobility
- It has less features
- There was still a limit to the number of users

2.5G and 2.75G system

Briefly, in the bid of supporting data rate, there was the General Packet Radio Service (GPRS). This was capable of data rate up to about 171kbps.

There was also the development of EDGE. This is the Enhanced Data GSM Evolution, which was able to improve data rate for GSM networks. It had a maximum speed of 473.6kbps

Subsequent to EDGE, there was also the CDMA200, which supported higher rates on the CDMA networks. With this technology, data rate climbed up to 384 kbps.

3G – Third Generation

This generation of network began with the introduction of the UMTS (Universal Mobile Terrestrial/ Telecommunication Systems). This generation was able to support vide calls, as it operated at a rate of 384kbps.

It was after the release of the 3G that we had smartphones become popular in the world. The smartphones were designed to handle tasks like the multimedia message, email, video calls, games, social media and other advanced functions.

Features of 3G

- There is an increased data rate
- It supported video calling
- There is enhanced security
- It was able to support mobile app
- There was also support for multimedia messages

- It supported tracking of location as well as maps.
- It offered better web browsing
- TV streaming
- It supported high quality 3D games

3.5G to 3.75 Systems

There were two subsequent developments to the 3G network. It was sort of a development, as the 3.5G network was able to support up to 2mbps data rate. The 3.75 system also offered more speed. There was the ultimate development of the 3.9G system, which is also known as the LTE (Long term Evolution).

Disadvantages of 3G

- It had a very expensive spectrum license
- The infrastructures were very costly
- It needed higher bandwidth for proper data rate support
- The mobile devices that supported it were very costly

4G – Fourth Generation communication system

This is the enhanced version of the 3G, it offered higher data rate and it was able to handle better multimedia functions. It was very easy to deploy as it was compatible with devices that supported the previous communication system generations.

Data rate is highly improved in the 4G, which aided the simultaneous transfer of video and audio data. The IP packets of the 4G is able to transfer any form of services. Transmission technologies like the WiMax was introduced on the 4G system. This enhanced the rate of data, as well as the performance of network.

Features

- Data rate could reach up to 1Gbps
- It features enhanced security and mobility
- There is a drastic reduction in latency
- It supported higher definition video streaming and gaming

Disadvantages

- It needed expensive hardware and infrastructure to run
- The spectrums were very costly
- Global deployment of the technology has proven to be time consuming.

5G – Fifth Generation Communication System

This is a proposed wireless communication network undergoing development. The establishment of the network has begun in some part of the world, and it is being designed to deliver ultra-fast internet and multimedia experience for users.

In the case of the 5G, millimeter waves and unlicensed spectrum will be used for the transmission of data. This is a massive data rate to be experienced, and to enable the use of this for internet of things, a complex modulation technique is being developed.

Another feature of the 5G is the cloud based network architecture. Cloud computing has become a thing in the world, and its astounding benefits are being leveraged in the development of the next generation cellular network. Cloud computing will increase it functionalities and analytical capabilities.

Features of the 5G

- Internet data speed can reach 10Gbps
- There is reduced latency even in milliseconds
- There is a reduction in data cost
- It provided higher security and a reliable network
- It makes use of technologies like small cells, this brings about improved efficiency
- The cloud based architecture offers it more power efficiency, maintenance and easy hardware upgrades.

As it stands, there seem to be no downside to the use of 5G. However, this isn't ruled out just yet. 5G offers so much benefits to the cellular communication, and the possibilities with it in other areas of technology is simply unimaginable.

Cellular System Architecture

The architecture of the cellular system is as basic as it can get. There are three main parts that constitute, which are;

-   A network of cells, of which each has its base station
-   A packet switched network that is used for communication between the mobile switching centers and the base stations
-   The Public switched telephone network: it serves the function of connecting subscribers to the wider network of telephone users

Mobile switching centers

This is a network switching subsystem which belongs to a cellular phone system. This is also referred to as the mobile telephone switching office (MTSO). One unique feature of the MTSO is the fact that all base stations are connected to an MSC. The MSC has the following functions

-   It fosters the setup of calls as well as their release
-   It helps with routing of calls and messages that are sent via SMS
-   It is used in the management of conference calls and calls left on hold
-   It is also used for fax services
-   It is used in billing

- It is used in interfacing with other networks.

This explains the basic architecture of the cellular network

Elements of a Communication System

What do you know about communication, either between a person and computer or between a computer and another computer? Communication between components didn't just come to be, there are elements that work in sync to make sure it is possible. There are different types of communication, which include; radio broadcasting, television broadcasting, radio telegraphy, mobile communication, computer communication, etc. Here are the basic components that make up the communication systems

Information source

Communication networks are designed to ensure that information is sent from a sender and received at the end of the receiver. For there to be communication, information source is important. It is where the information originates, without which there will be no communication in the first place.

The information emanating from the source may be sound, picture, words, etc. whenever you talk to someone over the phone, you are the information. In this case however, the information source is situated at both ends. It is a dialogue, and the sound is sent through the system whenever each responds.

Input transducer

During communication, sound is the information being sent. This however cannot transmitted over a long distance. In this case, there is a need for the sound to be transmitted into electrical signals or light signal. This is achieved by the transducer. When the information gets to the destination, it is then converted back to sound.

Basically, a transducer has the function of converting one form of energy to another. To make sure that sound in sent and received in real form, there is a transducer at both ends of the communication line. The output transducer simply converts the light energy back to sound energy.

Transmitter

In the communication system, there is the transmitter which is responsible for the conversion of signal produced at the source, into a form that can be transmitted through a channel. The main technique used by the transmitter is the modulation.

When the transducer converts the sound into electrical energy, the transmitter than through modulation converts it to a form that can be transmitted via the channel. This is basically the function of the transmitter – modulation.

Communication channel

This is the medium which fosters the transmission of a signal from one point to another. There are two main mediums of transmission, which can be wired or wireless. These has been extensively explained in the course of this book, you can refer it if you need to refresh your memory.

Noise

Noise is a phenomenon in which signals that are unwanted find their way into a communication system. This interferes with the signal being transmitted. When this occurs, there is a degradation of transmitted signals.

Receiver

This is the component of the communication network that receives the signal being transmitted. It converts the transmitted signal back to its original form.

Output transducer

The transducer is the one present on the output part of a communication network. In most cases, the output transducer works to convert electrical signals into a non-electrical signal. One of the most common form of the output transducer is the loudspeaker.

Destination

This is the final stage of the communication system. In most cases, humans are always the destination of a particular communication string. Where the information sent is being consumed is called the destination.

Messaging systems: Electronic Mail and Voice Processing

Messaging has become a really important part of human communication, especially with instant messaging social media networks like Facebook, Telegram, Kik, etc. It has sufficed as an alternative to phone calls, as well as being the medium for official communications between corporate persons and the public.

A messaging system can be defined as one designed to foster the transmission of text messages from one user to another user. There are messaging systems that have been developed to support the transfer of pictures, videos and other forms of content, from one place to another. Basically, in the messaging system, electronic mail is also included, alongside text messaging and instant messaging.

In the messaging system, there are basic components that ensure the possibility of the various types of messaging.

- **Mail User Agent:** This is the email program of the client, such as Gmail, outlook, Eudora or Mac Mail. This is the program or application on the end of the user, used in the composition, transfer and reception of messages

- **Message transfer agent:** This is the part of the system that is responsible for the transfer of messages from the user. It also functions in delivering messages to its own message store, where it can be accessed by local recipients

There are two widely used Message Transfer Agents (MTA), which are Microsoft Exchange and Sendmail. However, for enterprise, there are several other formats of the MTA used.

- **Message Store:** This is the component that stores and holds incoming messages, till it is retrieved or deleted by the user. From the MTA to the Message store, a tool called the Local Delivery Agent ensure delivery of messages. In the retrieval of messages, two main protocols are used, which are; POP and IMAP.

- **Internet's SMTP:** Mail sent via the internet is based on the SMTP protocol. Prior to the growth of the internet in late 1990s, there were several messaging systems in use, which included; Microsoft Mail, PROFS and DISOSS.

Messaging has transformed the way we relay information between ourselves and other. Technological advancements had contributed immensely into making messaging a really good experience. In this section, we will be talking a look at two critical messaging systems that are deemed critical to the future of information. These are Electronic mail and Voice Messaging

Electronic Mail

The definition is pretty simple. Electronic mail is a digital framework that supports the exchange of messages via the internet or intranet communication platforms. Electronic mail is also shortened to E-mail. It's sort of writing a letter but the only difference here is that, rather than using a pen, you make use of keyboard. In most cases now, with the text-to-speech technologies, you can write an email message, just by speaking to your device.

The structure of the email address is somewhat unique. In that, it consists of a custom username at the beginning, which is followed by the domain name of the service provider, with the "@" separating the two.

What can email be used for?

The use of email has become ubiquitous. In fact, over 290 billion emails are sent daily, and the reasons for these are just the benefits that comes with its use

- **It is very fast:** Emails can be sent fast and delivered without a lag in time. This is one reason why it has become really popular, especially for enterprises.

You can communicate with anyone just within your building, or across the length of the world.

- **It is very convenient:** in fact, in many cases where you could have placed a call, you can simply send a mail. If you have a quick enquiry about something and what to save yourself the time of having to get familiar over calls, then explaining what you want, a summarized mail can get you the answer pretty quick.

- **You can send attachments:** With the email, you can send documents attached. You can attach files like videos, pictures, pdfs, word documents, etc.

- **It is easily accessible:** On your email account, you can have files and messages stored up, which can sift through easily and access at any point you want them. Just a type in Google's Gmail will take you to the particular message you are after. It is that easy to use.

- **It serves as a record:** And for conversations where it would be better to have a documentation, it is better to use emails rather than phone calls. You can easily go back to conversations whenever you want them.

- **There is no limit to writing space:** With the SMS, there is a limit to the space you have to write. However, with the email, you can write as much as you want. You can pour all your heart out, or sell yourself as much as you want, or file complaints of whatever length. You can do any length of text with emails.

- **It is secure:** There are special emails designed to be as secure as possible. Special privacy and security protocols deployed to make sure confidential and sensitive information are kept safe.

Short comings of the Email

Well, there is one major problem to email, which annoys many users. This is spam. There are several junk emails that find its way into your mail box, and in the process, really important messages can be lost. This problem however is being tackled, but not yet perfect.

Email service providers now make use of filters that sift through the various mails coming in, picking out the relevant ones from the bunch of irrelevances. As said, it isn't perfect yet, as some spam mails still find their way to your mail box.

Speech Processing

There are two main concepts of speech processing. It involves the study of speech signals. It also involves the methods involved in processing of signals. These signals are processed digitally, hence you can refer to the process as a form of digital signal processing. There are various aspects involved in speech processing. These include; acquisition, manipulation, storage, transfer and output of speech signals. The process involved in imputing sound is called speech recognition, while the output is called speech synthesis.

Techniques of Speech Processing

There are three main techniques used in speech processing, which are;

- **Dynamic Time Warping**

This is shortened as DTW, and it is an algorithm that used in the measurement of existent similarities between two mundane sequences, which vary with respect to speed. Generally, you can refer to DTW as a process that calculates how optimally matched two sequences are. This measurement is executed within some restrictions and rules.

The match that satisfies the rules and restrictions at low cost, is referred to as the optimal match.

- **Hidden Markov Models**

This is the most basic of the dynamic Bayesian network. The algorithm has the primary goal of estimating the hidden variable that has been allotted to a list of observations.

- **Artificial Neural Networks**

The Artificial Neural Network is a system based on the connection of nodes and units that are referred to as artificial neurons. The artificial neurons are somewhat the replica of the neurons situated in the human brain. Each connection in the ANN can transmit signal from one neuron to the other.

Speech processing as a technological breakthrough has since advent being employed in various ways. It is fundamentally used in interactive voice systems, virtual assistants, voice identification, emotion recognition, call center automation and robotics. Many of these cases are still not full developed to offer real time processing, but it is close. In the case of virtual assistants, assistants like Google assistant are optimized to offer real time processing.

Fundamentals of data communication

Communication is a basic need of life. Life scientists refer to us as social animals (though I prefer to be called a social being), and this means we need to reach out to one another. Communication technologies over the years has helped us maximize this. It has enhanced the way, speed and quality of how we reach out to ourselves. There are four fundamentals that data communications stick to.

- **Delivery:** This is the concept which dictates that every data communication system is able to deliver data to the right destination, at every instance. The data sent out must always be received by the intended recipient.
- **Accuracy:** There must be no loss of components in the data being sent. It must be delivered accurately. This is because data been altered during transmission without correction, is rendered unusable.

- **Timeliness:** Real-time is the standard. Data being sent should be delivered as timely as possible. When data is delivered late, it becomes useless. When it comes to video and audio, timeliness means having the data delivered as soon as it is produced. The data should be delivered as soon as it is produced, in the order in which it was produced, and without delay. This is what we refer to as real-time data transmission.

- **Jitter:** The word jitter is used in referring to variation in the arrival time of data packets. This is most experienced when video is to be delivered. In this case, there is a variation in the delivery of the audio packets of the data, against the video packets. Jitter can also occur in a particular format. Such that, in a video transmission, some parts of the video may arrive at 3D-ms, while others lag and arrive at 4D-ms. This causes a disruption in the video quality.

Public Switched Telephone Network (PSTN)

PSTN is a combination of an interconnected telephone line network, which is co-owned by government and private owners. This network system actually has been in use from the 1800s, and it made use of underground copper wires. The use of these over the last decade has been on a decline, as wireless communication takes over the world.

Properties of PSTN

- It is also termed the Plain Telephone Service (POTS)
- The concept evolved from the invention of the telephone by Graham Bell
- It has the main function of transferring voice in relatable form
- It is a combination of several circuit-switched across the world
- It started by laying copper across the whole area it covered, it has evolved from that.

Communication of information, news and other events has become easier over the past decade. Engineers, researchers, developers and many other technically-oriented personnel has worked assiduously in ensuring that the world is connected. The cellular networks are a revolutionary breakthrough, and it has changed the way things operated in the world. Imagine how hard it would be, if to reach out to a relative in Australia, we still needed to send a letter from America, then wait for a response, before sending a follow up. It would take years to complete quite a handful of conversations.

Communication networks are used extensively in the world of today. It is used in communicating with astronauts in space, planes in airfields, ships in the middle of the sea, etc.

Chapter 10: Wireless Network Technology and its Utilities

Wireless Network Technologies has so many principles which aids implementation, and this is a pretty wide area of computer networking concept. It is the wireless network technologies that has made it possible for wireless network to be adopted to various devices, and for different uses. These technologies have been adapted for use, both at home and in different business networks. Wireless network has come with both its upside and downside, just like any other technology out there. In the course of this book, we have tried to establish the fact that wireless network is what has made the world better than it used to. We need wireless networks, irrespective of the limitations it suffers.

There are several technologies put in place to make wireless networks possible, and those are what we will be examining in this chapter of the book.

What is CISCO systems?

You probably must have heard of CISCO in the computer networking world (that's if you are not a novice – consumers only). Cisco systems, Inc. is one of the leading networking company in the world. The company started by the couple, Sandy Lerner and Len Bosack in 1984, is best known for being the leading manufacturer and seller of different networking equipment. Products from the company are however not limited to hardware, they also make software products and devices related to them.

Through its years of operation, the company has focused on providing software and other services based on the Internet Protocol (IP). They also focused on products for routing and switching. They also focus on other technologies used extensively for home networking, IP telephony, optical networking, security, storage area networking and wireless technology.

The couple who met at Stanford University are since divorced, but the first product developed by their company had been the AGS router, developed by Bosack and Kirk Lougheed.

The various applications and products developed by Cisco are all adaptable for tablets, mobile phones, desktop virtualization and many more.

The company as a whole makes provision of security services and products. These features are known to offer network, identity, and security to contents. These tools have been in effective in helping clients reduce the theft of their data. With the various tools, clients are also able to work in a collaborative and cloud-enabled environment.

The market of Cisco had been greatly competed by the likes of HP, Avaya, Juniper, etc. But the company has been able to ensure dominance. In computer networking, Cisco was able to develop a switch, called the Catalyst 6500. This has been adopted for use in submarines and mountaintops.

They also made the CR-3 routing system, which has been labelled as being so powerful to stream all of the motion pictures captured in less than four minutes. The system is also so fast that it can have all the printed collection in the library of congress, all done in just about 1 second.

Let's take a look at the various products by Cisco

Cisco Routers for Home

For 10 years, spanning between 2003 and 2013, Cisco was the parent company of Linksys (both the business and the brand name). Linksys as a company was involved in making wired and wireless router models, which suddenly became popular for networking in the homes. However, Linksys got sold to Belkin.

Cisco Routers and the Internet

In the early days of the internet, Cisco routers were used in building a long-distance connection. This was between the 1980s and 1990s. The piece of tech back then was not used for just long distance connections, it was used by enterprise to create intranet networks.

Cisco CSR – Carrier Routing Systems

These were created to function as routers, and they served as the very core of large enterprise networks. To this component of the network, you can connect routers and switches. It was first introduced in 2004, and it offered 40 Gbps connection. It also featured a network bandwidth that can be scaled to about 92 terabits per second.

Cisco ASR – Aggregation Service Routers

These are EDGE routers, and they were designed serve as interface between an enterprise's network and the internet. It can also interface the enterprise network with another Wide Area Network.

Cisco ISR – Integrated Services Routers

There are three series in this line up, and they include the 1900, 2900 and 3900 series Cisco.

Cisco IOS – Internetwork Operating System

This is a low-level network software that was designed to run on the Cisco routers. It could also run on other Cisco devices. It basically supports a command-line user interface shell. There were two variations of the IOS, which are the IOS XE and the IOS XR. There is no difference to these and the flagship

Cisco IOS, they only added additional features not on the Cisco IOS.

CISCO Network Certifications

The Network Certification programs by CISCO are recognized across the world, and these certifications are available at different levels.

Entry Level (CCENT & CCT)

There are two main certifications possible in the Entry Level category. These are the CCENT and the CCT. These are designed for enthusiasts who are new to the trade, and are just starting a career in Computer Networking. These certifications require no prerequisites. The study materials for the entry level certifications can be acquired online, and the certification only comes after the registered individual has passed the examination.

With this certification, the individual becomes a professional who can install, maintain and troubleshoot small networks. They are also able to perform all these functions on the branch of an enterprise network.

The entry level is also prerequisite for some associate-level CCNA solution track credentials.

For the CCT professional, the main function is to work on-site at customer locations. They are saddled with the primary responsibility of diagnosing issues, subsequently performing repair functions. When one is certified with CCT, progress can be made in Data Center and Routing and Switching.

Associate Level (CCNA & CCDA)

There are also two certifications in this category. Which are the Cisco Certified Network Associate (CCNA) and Cisco Certified Design Associate (CCDA). To receive this certificate, the individual must pass about two exams.

In this certification, basic functions like installation, support, and troubleshooting can be performed on both wired and wireless networks. There are several career tracks available to the associate level professional. These include; Cloud, Collaboration, Cyber ops, data center, industrial, routing and switching, security, service provider and wireless.

The CCNA is the prerequisite to the professional level CCNP. The Prerequisite to study the CCNA is all dependent on the career track chosen by the individual.

This certification was designed by Cisco to hand pick individual that are capable of basic wired design, as well as wireless networks.

For the CCDP (Cisco Certified Design Professional), the CCDA is a prerequisite. However, for individuals to obtain the CCDA, CCENT, CCNA (routing and Switching), coupled with an additional exam, are required.

Cisco Professional Level Certifications (CCNP & CCDP)

For the Cisco professional-level certificates, there are two main programs; the Cisco Certified Network Professional (CCNP) and Cisco Certified Design Professional (CCDP). To obtain the CCDP certification, the individual needs to pass three examinations, and fulfil the prerequisites of CCDA and CCNA (routing and switching)

All the solution tracks in CCNP require that participants is subjected to four examination, except the Routing and Switching track. For the routing and switching, three exams are pertinent.

For the CCNP solution tracks, there is a prerequisite of either of the lower-level CCNA or CCIE credentials. For the CCNP service provider credential, candidates can also possess the Cisco Certified Internet Professional (CCIP) credential.

Once an individual is certified with the CCNP, he is recognized as being able to handle the planning, deployment and troubleshooting of local networks and wide area networks. There is no difference in the tracks of CCNP and CCNA. This is the requirement except in the industrial design and Cyber ops track. These however are not offered in the CCNP tracks.

Any professional who wants to be certified with the Cisco Certified Internetwork Expert must possess the CCNP. Individuals with the CCDP are able to design and deploy scalable networks, as well as other multilayer-switched networks.

Cisco's Expert-Level Certifications (CCIE & CCDE)

There are two primary certifications embraced by the Cisco Expert-level credentials. These are the Cisco certified internetwork expert (CCIE) and the Cisco Certified Design Expert (CCDE). For these certifications, there are no compulsory prerequisites. However, you need to pass an examination, and the practical sessions are very strict.

As of 206, there was an update to the Cisco Expert-level exams, causing it to include an evolving technologies domain. With the new domain, the target is now cloud, programmability of network and internet of things. This accounts for 10 percent of the total exam score.

The main concept of this new domain is that the topics can be changed easily, to adapt to evolving technologies. This is a way in which the certifications remain valid, as it helps participants stay up-to-date with technology.

The CCIE has several tracks which include; collaboration, data center, routing and switching, security, service provider and wireless.

For the CCDE, experts can design infrastructure solutions for large enterprise environments. These environments include; technology, operations, business and budgeting.

Cisco's Architect-Level Certifications

This is the best network for professionals looking to attain the level of network architects. They can also be data center architects. The Cisco Certified Architect certification (CCAr) is just like the Ph.D of the Cisco certifications. This is the highest level of certification offered by Cisco.

Experts with this certificate are able to plan and design IT infrastructures that are based on specific business strategies. For many people, this is the most difficult tech certification to achieve. To be sincere, it is arguably the most difficult to attain.

One of the prerequisites to obtaining this certification is to design a network solution that will implement and assigned strategy. When this is done, the individual needs to appear before a Cisco-appointed panel. At this presentation, the individual needs to defend the solution he had created.

Job Opportunities for the various Certifications

- CCENT: They can easily get jobs at help desks or some other technical roles.

- CCT: Can serve as engineers or as a system administrator.

- CCNA: The individual can serve as an engineer, a technician or an analyst.

- CCDA: Professionals at this certification level serve as engineers, interface developers or technical specialists

- CCNP: Can serve as a network administrator, and engineer or as an advanced technician. They can also take up some senior-level roles

- CCDP: They take up senior-level roles, such as senior network design engineer, senior analyst, cyber protection analyst or a network designer.

- CCIE: They can take up expert level roles, which include; network architects, engineers or senior network administrator

- CCAr: Architects.

Cisco Packet Tracers

This is a cross-platform visual simulation tool that was brought into design and implementation by Cisco. This tool allows users to create network topologies, in the bid of creating new computer networks. With this software, users can use a simulated command line interface to simulate the configuration of routers made by Cisco, as well as switches.

The user interface for Cisco packet tracer is sort of a drag and drop model. This way, users, can add or remove devices from the network, as they deem fit. This software is mainly used by students of the associate level certifications by Cisco. It helped them learn the very basics of the CCNA concepts.

This software can be run on the Linux, Windows and macOS. The app is also available on both iOS and Android devices.

The Cisco system and tools have been very instrumental in redefining computer networking, and making it what it is today. This has established the company as an authority in the field, making their certification recognizable wherever it is presented.

Hey! The book is not ended yet, you know?

Chapter 11: Differences Between Wired and Wireless Networks

In the course of this book, we have looked extensively at the various aspects of the wired and wireless networks. We have seen all the components, the uses, the applications, etc. All these are sure to have exposed you to all that the two types of computer networking are. This section is simply to bring your mind to the consciousness of what the two systems stand for.

Wired networks

As said earlier, a network can only be called wired if there is the possibility of a wireless of it being wireless. Wired networks is used in the description of network setups which involve the use of physical cables in the transfer of data between devices connected across ends. The cables used in this case are mostly made of copper, and can be a twisted or a fiber optic.

The wired networks convey electrical signals from one end to the other. In most of the wired networks, Ethernet cables are used in the transfer of data between computers connected one to another. However, for Ethernet, the range it can reach is very limited, and the configuration is also not as easy as that of the wireless networks.

Wireless networks

For the wireless networks, it makes use of infrared and radio frequency in the sharing of information as well as resources. This design was borne out of the need to cut down on what is needed to ensure connection of devices. It has eliminated the problem of distance and obstacles.

There is a total elimination of the use of wires in the case of the wireless networks. As said earlier, it makes use of radio waves. Many devices in existence today make use of this technology; cellular, handhelds, satellite receivers, laptops, PDAs and wireless sensors.

Table of Comparison

The table below outlines the various parameters involved in computer networking

S/n	Parameters	Wired Network	Wireless Network
1	Installation	It is more difficult to install the wired network than it is for	Installation is easier for the wireless network

		the wireless network due to number of components needed.	
2	Speed and Bandwidth	It has a very high speed	It has a lower speed
3	Reliability	It is more reliable due to performance	Reliability is reasonably high
4	Cables	Ethernet, copper and optical fibers	It works with radio waves and microwaves
5	Mobility	Devices connected to on the wired network cannot be moved	There is no limitation to its mobility

		around easily	
6	Security	It has a really good security	Security is weak and network can be compromised by hackers
7	Interference	There is next to no interference experienced with the wired networks	It is prone to high interference
8	Quality of service	The quality of service is better as compared to the wireless networks	Quality of service is low
9	Setup time	Setup takes less time	Setting up and connecting the

			components takes time	
10	1	Devices used	Hubs and switches are used	Routers are used in this case
11	1	Cost	The total cost of installation are now lower, since cables are cheaper	Since there is an increase in demand, the prices of components are very high.
12	1	Applications	LAN, MAN	WLAN, WPAN (Zigbee, Bluetooth), Infrared, Cellular (GSM, CDMA)
13	1	Standards	IEEE802.3	IEEE802.11a, IEEE802.11b, IEEE802.11g

The wired and wireless networks will persist, with each adapted to their strengths. Of course, till the wireless networks can effectively surpass the wired networks in areas of its strength, there will always be the wired networks.

Chapter 12: Computer Network Security

One thing became synonymous with the wireless networks – hacks! Here and there, you hear of cases of data being compromised and unauthorized individuals finding their way into computer networks. This is no news in the cyberspace. In fact, according to the official annual cybercrime, it is estimated that cybercrime will cost us about $6 trillion by 2021. As of 2015, we suffered from $3 trillion being lost to cybercrime. This is to tell you how much you need to secure computer networks you engineer.

There is no point structuring a system and it can be easily compromised. When it comes to cybercrime, not only money is involved. There is the theft of data, information, access and many other things unauthorized crave to do on your system.

Earlier in this book, we have discussed the various security protocols we have and how best they can be used. In this chapter, we will take a further look at the security problems your computer network is bound to face, and how best you can tackle them. Hackers are always on the watch, and are ready to compromise a system if the management slacks for a bit. There is so much to know about the security of your computer network, and it's only right to pay close attention as we move through all you need to know.

Common Security Threats

Security issues faced by computer networks are massive. Computer networks are prone to facing several advanced problems that can force a shutdown, however, let's take a quick look at basic security threats a computer network faces

Computer Virus

There is arguably no one in the world that can lay claim to the fact that they don't know what a virus is. It is a plague that has affected several personal computers, as well as computer networks. Especially if you make use of the internet, viruses are the easiest way for your computer to get damaged. According to reports, about 33% of household computers get affected by malware of one type or the other.

Viruses are simply software that spread across a computer network, which go on to corrupt and destroy data stored on the system. Viruses are known to find their way into the computer system, either through email attachments, or they are downloaded mistakenly. They can also find their way into the systems via USB, or other cables connected from another device.

Rogue security software

This is a new technique with which scammers and digital hackers find their way into the computer system.

The system of hacking takes advantage of people's fear of viruses. They offer virus solutions, and once you accept the offer, it leads to your system being compromised. They either tell you that your system is infected with a virus, or you should pay for a tool to protect your system. Either way, it's only a trick to disrupt the functioning of your system.

Trojan horse

Remember the case of the Trojan horse in Troy? This is the concept represented here. It is simply a situation in which a malware hides behind legitimate software, to find its way into the system. In fact, this may come in as email from people you know. Once you click on the attachment, the malware finds its way into your computer.

Once this virus finds its way into your computer, it can save your password by logging the various keystrokes. It can also compromise your webcam, or cart away a copy of sensitive data stored on the system.

Phishing

This process is similar to that of the Trojan horse. It is a social engineering method, which has an ultimate goal of collecting passwords, usernames and credit card numbers. The software comes in the form of legitimate mails, but when downloaded to the computer, they are automatically installed.

DOS and DDOS attack

DOS means Denial of Service, while DDOS means Distributed Denial of Service. DOS is such that, a particular server based website is attacked simultaneously by traffic from a particular computer. This causes the server of the website to experience downtime, as it becomes overloaded. It simply works by a single computer IP loading out different packets on to a particular web address, rather than a single packet. This system of attack can easily be traced, and intercepted, hence, there is the evolution of DDOS.

In the case of the DDOS, rather than a single computer being used, it makes use of different computers, which could number from just 2 to thousands. This is more difficult to stop and more lethal.

Rootkit

This is a combination of software tools which can grant a user administration-level access over a particular network. Once this access is secured, the malware situated in the collection carry out various compromising activities on the computer or network. In this collection, there are key loggers, password stealers and antivirus disablers.

Rootkits have a basic way of functioning, just like the Trojan horse security threat. It comes with a legitimate software, which requires changes to your OS. Once this installation is done, the rootkit installs itself and awaits activation from the hacker.

SQL Injection attack

Storage servers for websites and app mainly use SQL. To compromise this system, there is the evolution of the SQL injection attacks. These attacks are designed to target applications that make use of data. Any loophole found in the systems on which such application is hosted, is exploited. This is one of the most dreaded threat to computer systems in recent times.

Man-in-the-middle attacks

This is a sort of network compromise, in which the hacker can listen in on users. If there are two targets, the hackers are able to eavesdrop on the communication line between both. These conversations normally should be private and/or encrypted, however, this breaches that.

How do network viruses spread?

Spreading of viruses on computers can be so spontaneous, as it can occur via email attachments, boot infections and program infectors. These are simply the basic ways in which viruses spread on the computer. There are other lethal processes through which viruses spread.

- **Infection from network**

There are different types of the computer networks, and the way viruses spread on the different types are similar. The basic purpose of the various networks is to share software and other information between two or more computers. Over networks, there is the sharing of files, and in this process, there is the possibility of viruses being shared with the files.

In recent times, the common cyber-attacks have been targeted towards big tech companies. This is in the bid of disrupting their services. In most of these cases, DOS is employed. This functions in such a way that, the hackers have viruses infected across computers of various users. Then at a specific time, there is a launch of the combined attack towards the target.

During these hacks, users will notice that their computers perform some activities without their knowledge.

In defense of these attacks, firewalls are to be used. With an advanced up-to-date firewalls, launching these attacks becomes more difficult.

- **Other infection processes**

One major way in which viruses spread is by the download of software from software patches, drivers and demonstration software. The internet is littered with several software, most of which have been designed to execute these malicious processes.

Other than software, emails are another easy way hackers find their way into systems. Emails and other messaging platforms are very effective for the sharing of information and resources. However, their use have been undermined to aid the transmission and re-transmission of infections.

Computers with Internet explorer or outlook express are the most affected. This is because they are the most used in the world, and have several default permissions enabled in the computer. This creates an easy path for the virus as well as a template around the computer.

Signs of Viral Attacks on Computers

The very first step in protecting your computer from viral attacks is to know when it is suffering from a viral attack. You can't fight what you don't know. Viral attacks can be pretty to detect when the effects are in advanced stages, at which point, it may be difficult to protect the computer unscathed. There are some signs to look out for, which will tell if your computer is compromised.

- **Pop-up windows:** When you notice pop ups that shouldn't be there on your computer, it is one of two things – or both. The best thing to do in this case is to make sure you don't click on the pop-up ads. There is probably malware lurking behind the ad.

- **There is a reduction in performance:** When a system is infected by virus, the processes on it are slowed down, especially the start up. Though when you notice your computer slowing down, you need to confirm if the problem is with the RAM or the memory. If it is not, it is most likely the effect of a virus.

- **Suddenly exhaustion of storage space:** When you suddenly notice that the storage in your computer is exhausted, and you can't really trace any document or file taking up space, it is most likely a virus.

- **Missing files:** Malwares are known to cause problems, especially as files end up missing on the computer. There are some cases in which the files are there, but they are encrypted. It is viruses in action in this case too.

- **Error messages:** Whenever you notice the indiscriminate opening and closing of programs, then the system is infected with virus.

- **Hijacked email:** Viruses are an easy way to hijack emails, and when you notice this, making a report to the service provider is best.

- **High network activity:** There are cases in which the internet activities are on the high, even when the tabs on the browser or apps are not opened. In this case, it is most likely the virus sending information and data to the hacker's location.

How to prevent your computer from viruses

Viruses are real, and if you are not proactive in your dealing with them, it can cost you more. One of the best ways to deal with viruses is by being proactive in the protection of your computer. Cybercrime with the aid of viruses are getting rampant. It like wild fire, and many hackers are leveraging on the destructive ability of viruses to find their way into whatever systems. You need to beware, and your data, information and money protected. Here are some preventive measures you can adopt to make your computer safe from viruses.

- **Install quality antivirus:** Free anti-virus software will never be enough. One thing you should know about viruses is that, they are constantly evolving. Newer virus versions are always created, to beat the security against older viruses. To have access to premium anti-virus protection, you need pay. Getting quality anti-virus protection is very important. Especially if you are one who is always online or connects to different devices all the time.

- **Scan your computer daily:** I don't believe you should leave your anti-virus idle on the computer. Having paid for it, you need to maximize. Scan your computer daily. Viruses can find their way into the computer at any time, and causing extensive takes variable periods. To stay secure, perform a proper scan of the computer daily.

- **Disable autorun:** As explained earlier in this chapter, one of the ways in which anti-virus find their ways into computers is by installing themselves. They come into the system disguised as another app, they drive themselves to running. To combat this, you need to disable to autorun feature on your computer.

- **For mails, disable automatic image preview:** In your email setting, make sure you have preview disabled. By previewing images, the file is processed by your computer. In the course of this, the virus can find its way into your computer even before you open the mail. Be on the safer side.

- **Beware of sites you visit:** Some websites are stocked with malware, and other vices of whatever type. You need to be careful of sites you go, especially when those sites are labelled not secured by your browser. You can also combat this by making use of premium anti-virus software. These will check through links you click on, and ensure the credibility.

- **Use a hardware-based firewall:** There are viruses that are capable of disabling software-based firewalls. This can occur when devices are being shared or network resources are being jointly used. In this case, the software firewall installed on windows is simply not enough. In that case, it is best to get protected by hardware-based firewalls.

- **Use DNS protection:** Getting connected to the internet poses a lot of risk. There are some websites that spread infected programs, applications and Trojan files. There are also cases of DNS attacks, or compromised

DNS servers. These amongst others are what you are prone to on the internet.

Spywares

Spywares are a bit different from virus, though, they have the same underlining mission of compromising your computer system. However, spyware is a type of software which is designed to grant access to your computer without your consent. Most of these spyware are meant to undermine the computer of its information and data. There are different types of spyware, with each of them having different mission in your computer. It is best to know what they are all about, don't you think. You can't fight what you don't know.

Types of spyware

- **Adware:** This form of spyware is mainly used by advertisers. When you visit a website this spyware records your behavior online, and it uses that information to know what you will be interested in, or not. This way, ads are more targeted towards you.
- **Keyboard logger:** This software is mainly used by hackers. When they need to get information on data you enter to different personal accounts, they use the keyboard logger. Whenever it's time to input sensitive information, probably when you are trying to access your online accounts, the spyware records whatever you

type on your keyboard. This is then transferred to the hackers, who get unauthorized access to your accounts.

- **Modem hijacker:** These persons find their way into your phone line, to make unauthorized calls, as well as grab as much information as they want. You won't know about all these activities, till it gets to those that cost you charges.

- **Browser hijacker:** This are spywares that are designed to restructure your homepage and bookmarks. Such that you are maliciously directed to a website you wouldn't have visited, ending up bombarded with ads, against your will.

- **Commercial spyware:** This is one case of authorized spyware. Because you actually agree to allow the spyware monitor you, so that you can access their services. However, the access given to the service is misused and ads are targeted at you.

How does spyware find its way to your computer?

Have you ever wondered how spyware find its way into our computers? Have you ever wondered if there is something you are missing? There are several ways with which spyware can find its way into your computer.

- **Drive-by download:** This is the process in which a website you are on, or a pop-up window suddenly wants to download and install spyware on your computer. There are cases where you get a warning for this action, and that is when your security systems are advanced, in the case where you don't have a strong security system, you will not even get a warning.

- **Piggybacked software installation:** This is the situation in which some applications during the process of their installation, installs spyware as part of the standard procedure. When you are not observant, you will end up installing others software than you bargained for.

- **Browser add-on:** These software are known to bring add-ons to your web browsers. They do this in addition to what they are promised to do. And in some cases, they simply perform the Trojan horse procedure of getting into the system.

- **Masquerades:** Of all the spyware infiltration procedures out there, this is the most lethal. This prove to you that they are designed to help you remove spyware. When you then install it to perform the function it says it will, it adds other spyware that damage the computer.

Zero-hour and Zero-day attacks

There are other security issues beyond just viruses and spywares. One of such if the zero-day vulnerability (or Zero-hour attacks). This is a flaw in software security, such that the developer is aware of an issue, but there is no patch or software in place to fix the flaw. In this case, the gap can be exploited by hackers.

This is called software vulnerability, and they are flaws that surface in software programs or the operating system of a computer. They can result from the bad configurations in the computer system. If this is not corrected easily, it gives hackers the time frame to operate and compromise the system.

In the case of the Zero-day attacks, the vulnerability is just discovered. In this case, there is no patch to solve the problem. They call this situation "zero-day" because there is no time for the developer to prepare for the attack, "Zero days."

When this issue makes its way to the mainstream, the service provider needs to find an immediate solution, to douse panic of the users and keep the system away from hackers.

How to protect your system from zero-day attacks

You don't want your system to be compromised by a zero-day attack. It can be an extensive damage to your data and computer. When it comes to securing your computer, you need to be proactive. You need to get premium anti-virus and anti-spyware installed on your system.

Also, whenever your legitimate anti-virus software needs an update, you need to do it immediately. This is because the update will protect your system from new and current vices, that the older version may not be able to protect you again.

Here are some tips of what you should be doing to protect you from zero-day attacks

• Make sure your software and security patches are up to date. You can ensure this by downloading the latest software.

• Analyze your online habit, and make sure you are safe and secure

• Make sure your security setting is configured to optimize your OS, the browser and your security software

• Get premium security software for maximum protection.

Hacker Attacks

I'm sure you are not new to what we refer to as cyber-attacks. That's most likely the fantasy of every kid who hold a computer and writes code in one language or the other. With the legendary hoodie attire, it seems cool to be a hacker. Well, not until one becomes a victim of hacker attacks.

Cyber-attacks are launched by criminals making use of one or more computers to compromise the network of a particular network. Cyber-attacks are known to disable or disrupt the functionality of computers and network. They are also launched to cart away with user data and information, and in some cases to compromise financial details of targets.

There are several processes through which cyber-attacks can be achieved. These include; malware, phishing, ransom ware, denial of service and others.

Types of Cyber-attacks.

There are several methods with which hackers can find their way into a computer system or network. These include; malware, phishing, SQL injection attack, Denial of service, man-in-the-middle attacks, credential reuse and Cross-site scripting.

Most of these have been described earlier in this book, hence, we will only be considering the latter two methods – credential reuse and cross-site scripting. In the cases that we have discussed, the attack is launched by the criminal, and when the computer network is compromised, they infiltrate to carry out their malicious activities.

- **Credential Reuse**

There are so many sites and other utilities we want to have access to, and simply need to login or create an account. In the midst of having access to all these information, users are mainly tempted to use the same credential across all platforms. Rather than having to enter unique passwords and usernames across various platforms, it is very tempting for users to use the same across these platforms. This is not a security best practice, but it is very handy, especially for people who have difficulty in remembering all the various numbers.

Hence, whenever a hacker is able to access a user's information on one compromised network, they are sure that the password is mostly retained on other platforms. Which will grant them user access. It is best that you make sure the passwords used across several platforms are different.

You don't need to worry about having to remember all the various passwords you use. You can make use of a password manager.

- **Cross-site scripting (XSS)**

This attack is similar to the SQL injection attack. In this attack, the criminal sources for several compromising codes, and injects them into a website. However, this codes are not targeted at the database of the website, they are only used to interface with the user. Hence, the site owner does not know if there is any problem. The vice simply runs on the browser of the user.

On that website, protocols and scripts that can automatically run are being targeted, such as the comment section. For example, a link to a malicious JavaScript can be written in the comment section. This places the information of the user risk, hence, undermining the credibility of the website.

Botnet

In the world of computer networks, botnets have proven to be of great threat and the number one issues of security systems. Once devices are interconnected, the probability that they can be infiltrated by botnets is very high.

How do they work?

The name is coined from two words, "robot" and "network". They are simply a network of robots that coordinated to perform comprising activities on the web. The administrators of these attacks with the botnets are referred to as "Botmasters or bot herders"

The extent to which the attack goes is all dependent on the size of the bot network. The wider the network, the more impactful the attack will be on the target. With the use of this system of hacking, the gain is mainly financial gains, or just the undermining of activities on the internet.

The botmasters control the bot army, and they bombard the target website, the traffic causes the website to shut down and stop functioning. This makes it impossible for legitimate users to access the network. This is a form of DOS or DDOS.

Botnet infection features

- They don't attack just one computer, they can be deployed to infect millions of computers.
- They are mainly deployed through the Trojan Horse virus.
- They can easily access and modify user's personal information
- The more complex forms of the botnets are capable of self-propagating
- They are very difficult to detect
- They take their time to steadily infiltrate a system, just waiting for the botmaster to issue a command.

Just about any network can be infiltrated by the botnet, once it is connected somehow to the internet. In fact, if you own a smart TV, refrigerator or microwave, it can be compromised with the use of a botnet.

Botnets can perform basic process and even more. In fact, there are several cases in which botnets are being sold on the internet. If a botmaster feels the need to dispose of the botnet, or have other hackers maximize it, he can sell it over the internet.

Botnet structures

There are two ways in which the botnet can be constructed, but each design is such that the master can maximize their activities.

- **Client-server model:** This is setup, such that there is a main server controlling the bots. In this case, control with the botmaster, who makes use of special software in the establishment and issuance of commands. This is called the command and control (C&C) server.

There are however some downsides to the use of this structure. The location of the botmaster can be easily determined by the law enforcement agency. Also, once the server is destroyed, the botnet is dead.

- **Peer-to-peer:** This is the system commonly in use now. In this case, the net of bots does not make use of a single server. The system is interconnected in the peer-to-peer structure. On every bot, there is a list of other bots, which they will seek when it's time for updates, or there needs to be the transmission of information.

With this structure of the botnet, it is very difficult for law enforcement to track down the initiator or crash the system. This system of bots is very difficult to disrupt.

How to prevent your network from botnet attack

By now, you should get the inkling that this is no minute attack. It is way different from the other types of cyber-attack, and you need to optimize the security of your system against it. Here are some ways you can save yourself from attack.

- Have your operating system updated
- Don't open email attachments from untrusted sources
- Don't download files from Peer-to-peer network, or other sites that share files.
- Have your anti-virus software up-to-date.

The need for security on a particular network of computers can never be over-emphasized. With the rise of the internet, and the interconnection that has been fostered by the wireless networks, it has become very easy for system to be compromised. The cases of cyber-attacks recorded is on the high, and you need to be more careful. Either with your personal computer, or the Local Area Network, or any other type of network, due care and pro-activeness must be ensured.

You can't be too careful. Be safe!

Chapter 13: Internet of Things.

Even if you weren't vying to find your way into computer networking, you will most likely have heard of internet of things. The term has become so common, that virtually everyone that uses the internet have heard of it. Well, there are many of these people that remain in the oblivion of what the concept really is about.

Various areas of life can be influenced with IoT, the boundaries are just limitless. There is so much we can achieve with IoT, and we would be talking about some of these in this brief chapter. If the coffee you got at the start of this book is exhausted, you should probably get more. Though, this isn't going to be a long boring read.

What exactly is Internet of things?

There is a simple definition to what the internet of things is. It is simply a description of the situation in which billions of devices in the world have access to the internet. These devices are connected to the internet, with the sole aims of collecting and sharing data. This ability of easily connecting physical devices to the internet is powered by cheap processors and wireless networks. Remember that in this book we spoke about wireless networks and IoT?

Normally, these devices would have been termed "dumb," but now, they are smart. That is the extent to which IoT can revolutionize our lives.

Just about any device out there can be connected to the internet. In fact, a whiz kid was able to connect a teddy bear to his computer, just because the bear had a system of recorded voice playing over an in-built speaker. Through the IoT concept, he was able to connect to the bear, and whatever voice he recorded through the microphone on his computer was played on the bear. This process bypassed what had been pre-programmed on the computer.

Another example. If you can switch on the light bulb in your house, just by using your smartphone that has an installed app, then it's an IoT system.

IoT can seem simple, like the pretty basic stuff. But, if the toys we have interacting with us are results of IoT, you should also know that a driverless autonomous truck functions based on IoT.

How does it work?

The functioning of IoT is very easy to understand. It functions by the sensors incorporated into the devices, which is able to connect to the internet, with the aim of integrating data from different devices, subject it to analysis and apply such information in solving local problems or performing tasks.

With the IoT devices, it is very easy to pinpoint what is useful and what is not. This way, patterns can be detected, recommendations can be made, and problems can be solved.

Having devices connected is a really great way of enhancing efficiency, and cutting down on accidents. Imagine if all cars can connect to one another when they are in certain range of each other, and if you are almost hit a car, the car can warn you that a car is fast coming just around the bend. That's pretty amazing. With information devices get from other devices they are connected to, they make smart decisions, which is one of the aims of technology. Right?

This tech is getting bigger than it was some years ago. In fact, in 2017, it was reported by Gartner that about 8.4 billion IoT devices were used in the world. There is estimation that this will be at 20.4 billion in 2020. The total spending on IoT amounted to $2trillion as of 2017. This is expected, with smart TVs and smart speakers being the main gadgets used in homes now.

Applications

There are several ways in which one can make use of the IoT. It is more than likely that you have used an IoT powered device and you just don't know. Let's take a look at some utilities that are being influenced by IoT. Notice I said "that are being." This is because IoT is real, as of now. It's not a concept of the future. I'm sure you know this anyways.

Internet of things and homes

This is one area that I'm pretty sure you have had a taste of IoT. If you have an Alexa powered home device, then you are on an IoT framework. This is such a promising area, such that big tech companies like Amazon, Google, Apple and Facebook are competing hard. Anyways, as of now, Amazon holds the forte in the design of smartphones.

There are several products in this light. Like the Amazon echo, the smart fridge, light bulbs, cameras, thermostats, etc. You can interact with all these devices without even having to be close to them.

Internet of things and smart cities

With the spread of censors just about every nook and cranny of a city, it is possible for government to know what is going on anywhere, in real-time. This is one of the key way in which IoT will be of really great advantage, in the near future.

With the different types of censors that can be deployed, such as cameras, environmental censors, etc. it becomes very easy to monitor what is going on in cities and know just how to respond in real time.

Internet of things and artificial intelligence

There is a single power to IoT, which is data. The framework has access to a large array of data. When all these data are collected in real time from different sources, and astutely analyzed, they can be used to make decisions that save lives.

This is where artificial intelligence comes in. IoT collects the data, store it, analyze it, then feed it to the A. when AI received this information from IoT, it uses it to make predictions.

One example of companies that extensively make use of this framework is Google. Oh, how I love that company. They hire the best people, and I love them for it. How then does Google combine the use of IoT and AI? It's pretty simple. The AI is used to manage the cooling system of the company's data center. In all tech companies, there are large space where data is stored in physical structures. In this data center, there are thousands of sensors.

These IoT sensors collect temperature information, and have them fed to the deep neural networks. This then makes predictions of how the future energy consumption will be. This has brought about efficiency in the management of the data center, and of course, it has reduced the number of people that needs to be employed to maintain the data center. There are two ways to this anyways. Some people mist have lost their job, or have a change of role when this happened, but that is a discussion beyond the scope of this book.

Internet of things: Security and Privacy

There is no kidding about this, one of the biggest issue with IoT right now, is security. IoT is able to source information from just about anywhere, but keeping itself safe has been a really big issue. When data is collected thanks to a particular sensor, maintaining the security of that data becomes a big issue. For data in transit, one would expect that there is something like encryption. Unfortunately, there is none. Even for data at rest, it is not as safe as it should be, and data could easily be compromised on the fickle network.

The IoT framework mostly can't be patched. Hence, they will continue being at risk, and it may be hard to control it. It's easy to bridge through people webcams and even home routers. In fact, with smart wristwatches, compromise comes easy. When this is done, the hacker can easily figure out the wearer's location, listen in on the user's conversations or even converse with him. This is absurd for a tech we hope will make our lives and cities smarter.

Basically, IoT is designed to be sort of the bridge between the digital world and physical life. Hence, when this can be easily compromised, the damage to both the physical and digital worlds can be extensive.

For example, if someone could hack into the cooling system monitoring IoT at Google, it could trick the AI system into making rash and wrong decisions, while it thinks extreme measures are needed.

Privacy is all about the protection of data, either in the form of video, audio and text. When this is compromised, it's unfair to users. There can be the illegal undermining of data, the tech companies supplying the IoT devices can also undermine data they have access to. They can sell the harvested data from the devices. They can also use it to target ads at you. Selling the device should be the primary business model of such companies. However, it is disturbing to know that the business model also maximizes he presence of data.

What is the future of IoT?

There is a geometric progression in the adoption of IoT. This is causing more companies with more ideas to spring up, hence, the prices of sensors and processors are dropping, all over the world. The main point here is, the make of IoT devices now costs less than it used to, and that's a good thing. IoT might not have the very drastic effect some other tech gadgets have, but in no distant future, it will be a basic utility, just like the mobile phones.

Conclusion

It's all about networks, it's all about the connection. It's just like human interaction. We need each other, communicating with each other, leveraging on individual knowledge, ideas and approach, that's how we got better as humans.

To ensure the effectiveness and efficiency in the use of computer, they need to be connected. That is the whole essence of computer networking. To foster the sharing of data and information across distances, as well as aiding the communication between individuals.

Computer networking has been around for ages, starting from the wired to the present wireless systems. We have been able to do justice to everything you need to kick start your knowledge of computer networking in this book. Getting familiar with the components and implementing your own networks should come easier.

I really hope the journey through the various aspects of computer networking has not being boring. It's awesome that you are here reading this book now.

It's not just about reading and knowing. The onus lies on you to implement and really kick off your own computer networking career. Tech is not moved by readers, it is moved by doers, and that is what you are. Just do it!